SPILLING THE BEANS
ON THE
CAT'S PYJAMAS

By the same author:

*i before e (except after c): old-school ways
to remember stuff*

*Remember, Remember (The Fifth of November):
The History of Britain in Bite-Sized Chunks*

SPILLING THE BEANS ON THE CAT'S PYJAMAS

Popular Expressions –
What They Mean and Where We Got Them

Judy Parkinson

Illustrations by
Louise Morgan

Michael O'Mara Books Limited

Published in Great Britain in 2009 by
Michael O'Mara Books Limited
9 Lion Yard
Tremadoc Road
London SW4 7NQ

New and revised edition

Formerly published, as *From Hue and Cry to Humble Pie: Curious,
Bizarre and Incomprehensible Expressions Explained*, in 2000 by Michael
O'Mara Books Limited; and as *Catchphrase, Slogan and Cliché: The
Origins and Meanings of Our Favourite Expressions* in 2003 by Michael
O'Mara Books Limited.

A CIP catalogue record for this book is available from the British Library.

Papers used by Michael O'Mara Books Limited are natural, recyclable
products made from wood grown in sustainable forests. The
manufacturing processes conform to the environmental regulations of the
country of origin.

ISBN: 978-1-84317-365-6

3 5 7 9 10 8 6 4

www.mombooks.com

With thanks to Chloe Rhodes.

Designed and typeset by K DESIGN, Somerset

Printed and bound in Great Britain by Clays Ltd, St Ives plc

FOREWORD

The English language has flourished over the centuries. Some turns of phrase are 'as old as Methuselah' – our ever-flexible language often revives phrases that we thought had 'bitten the dust' – and new words and expressions creep into the lexicon all the time. There's a different 'flavour of the month' for each generation.

So 'strike while the iron's hot': if you want 'to bone up' on the origins of some of the curiosities of the English language, 'take a dekko' through these pages and you'll be 'in seventh heaven'.

This book is 'the bee's knees', 'the cat's whiskers' and 'the cat's pyjamas', all rolled into one, as it 'spills the beans' on the origins of all these expressions and many more.

I will 'make no bones' about it and I won't 'beat about the bush' (after all, don't forget I'm 'talking turkey' here): this book contains some fascinating and remarkable stories about our best-loved and most colourful phrases.

The staples of our language – those familiar, well-worn expressions and clichés – originate from the most diverse sources. From the high street to Homer, from advertising to America, from army to air force, from stage to screen … it's an 'all-singing, all-dancing', round-the-world trip through our language's history.

If you've ever gone 'over the top', you can thank the armed forces. 'Walk the plank' and 'shake a leg' are both nautical terms, and I wouldn't be 'rubbing salt in the wound' to say that

that's another one. The world of sport, meanwhile, provides rich pickings. 'To throw in the sponge' and 'to come up to scratch' are both boxing terms, and American baseball has allowed us 'to take a rain check'.

But that's for another time. Look no further, you'll be 'as pleased as Punch'.

JUDY PARKINSON, 2009

ABOUT ONE'S EARS

This colloquialism, which means to be in a very bothersome situation in which one might sustain some pain or trouble, is a shortened form of the saying 'to bring a hornets' nest about one's ears'. A hornet is a type of large wasp, which can inflict a savage sting.

The expression 'to stir up a hornets' nest' implies the same degree of trouble as the phrase above – and suggests perhaps deliberate provocation too.

ACCORDING TO PLAN

A familiar expression that is frequently used ironically to describe things that did *not* go according to plan.

It derives from falsely upbeat communiqués issued during the First World War, often after a particularly bloody or shambolic operation; with the result that the phrase became associated with official attempts to cover up military incompetence and confusion.

Such inverted use of language creates a coded understanding between those 'in the know', strengthening the sense of camaraderie among those who suffer from such plans.

TO ACT THE GIDDY GOAT

To fool around. Goats are known for their unpredictable behaviour.

In the literal sense, 'giddy' means 'insane' or to be 'possessed by a god', but it has been used to mean 'silly' or 'foolish' since the early Middle Ages.

In Latin, 'goat' is caper; *goats are noted for their frisky nature. 'To cut a caper' means 'to skip or leap about playfully'.*

TO ADD INSULT TO INJURY

To hurt, by word or deed, someone who has already suffered an act of violence or injustice. The expression has been in use for centuries.

During the Augustan era, the so-called Golden Age of Latin literature (27 BC–AD 14), Phaedrus translated Aesop's (620–560 BC) fables into Latin verse, peppering them with anecdotes of his own. He quotes the fable about a bald man who tried to swat a fly that had bitten him on the head, but who missed the insect and instead gave his pate a sharp slap.

Whereupon the fly said, 'You wished to kill me for a mere touch. What will you do to yourself since you have added insult to injury?'

ALIVE AND KICKING

Active and in good health. The expression was coined in the late eighteenth century and probably referred originally to a healthy baby, either while still in the womb or just after birth.

Appropriately, *Live and Kicking* became the title of a popular Saturday-morning BBC TV children's show in the 1990s.

ALL CATS LOVE FISH, BUT FEAR TO WET THEIR PAWS

A traditional saying, dating back to at least the sixteenth century, used to describe a person who is keen to obtain something of value, but who is not bold enough to make the necessary effort or to take the risk.

It is to this saying that William Shakespeare (1564–1606) referred in *Macbeth* (1:7):

Letting 'I dare not' wait upon 'I would',
Like the poor cat i' the adage.

ALL GREEK TO ME

'It's all Greek to me' is used to mean that something is completely unintelligible to the speaker, Greek being a particularly tricky language to grasp because of its different alphabet.

It may have started out as an Anglicized version of the Latin phrase 'Graecum est; non legitur' meaning 'It is Greek; it cannot be read', which was often used by monk scribes in the Middle Ages, when Greek was falling out of use.

It was probably popularized by Shakespeare's *Julius Caesar* (1599), in which Casca says, 'For mine own part, it was Greek to me' (1:2).

ALL IN A DAY'S WORK

Said of an unusual or unexpected task that can be obligingly included in the normal daily routine.

The expression was common by the eighteenth century and may stem from the nautical use of the term 'day's work', which referred to the reckoning of a ship's course during the twenty-four-hour period from noon one day to noon the next.

A character in Sir Walter Scott's (1771–1832) novel *The Monastery* (1820) says, 'That will cost me a farther ride . . . but it is all in the day's work.'

ALL OVER BAR THE SHOUTING

This expression is firmly rooted in the world of sport and was first used in print by nineteenth-century sportswriter Charles James Apperley (1777–1843) in 1842. It means that victory is in the bag, only the cheering of the crowd at the end of the game or contest being lacking.

The phrase may perhaps be derived specifically from boxing – the shouting being the noisy appeal from the supporters of one of the boxers against the referee's decision.

It is also often applied to political elections in which the outcome is certain, even before the ballot papers have been counted.

> *In a famous reference to the phrase, an excited Kenneth Wolstenholme (1920–2002), the BBC's football commentator at the 1966 World Cup final at Wembley, said towards the end of the game, 'There are people on the pitch . . . they think it's all over.' He then added, as Geoff Hurst (1941–) scored a last goal for England – making the final score 4–2 and sealing the West Germans' fate – 'It is now!'*

ALL SINGING, ALL DANCING

This piece of popular phraseology was inspired by the first Hollywood musical, *Broadway Melody*, in 1929 – the era in which sound first came to the movies, which was advertised with posters proclaiming:

The New Wonder of the Screen!
ALL TALKING
ALL SINGING
ALL DANCING
Dramatic Sensation!

The phrase caught on immediately, and two rival studios used the same sales pitch in the same year for *Broadway Babes* and *Rio Rita*.

In about 1970, the computing world adopted the phrase to hype up new software, so that by the mid 1980s, every kind of organization seemed to boast that their computers and systems packages had some quality that was 'all singing, all dancing'.

Concurrently, the financial world embraced the phrase with enthusiasm to describe the stock market at the time of the 'Big Bang' (the major modernization of the London Stock Exchange that came into effect in October 1986).

Subsequently, the expression has been linked with anything from savings plans, pensions and mortgages to machines – especially electronically controlled machines – of almost any kind.

A saying with a similar meaning is the older phrase 'All bells and whistles', which also describes that all-important 'wow' factor.

ALL TARRED WITH THE SAME BRUSH

Everyone in the group shares the same failings; they're all sheep of the same flock. This old saying alludes to the methods used by farmers to mark their sheep. A brush dipped in tar was applied to the wool as a form of branding.

The phrase is now often used when people feel they have been lumped in with others and judged unfairly as a result.

ALL THAT GLITTERS IS NOT GOLD

Appearances are not what they seem. A saying that must have been in use for a thousand years or more and a favourite of poets, it is thought to be Latin in origin. It is a well-known note of prudence in Shakespeare's *The Merchant of Venice* (1596; 2:7):

> All that glisters is not gold,
> Often have you heard that told.

This implies that the proverb dates from earlier wisdom; certainly it was used by Geoffrey Chaucer (*c.*1343–1400) in *The Canterbury Tales*, for in 'The Canon's Yeoman's Tale' (*c.*1387), he wrote:

> However, all that glitters is not gold,
> And that's the truth as we're often told.[1]

Many other writers have referenced it, including Thomas Gray (1716–71) in his 'Ode on the Death of a Favourite Cat, Drowned in a Tub of Gold Fishes' (1747), but perhaps the most cynical use is that of Ogden Nash (1902–72), who observed in 'Look What You Did, Christopher':

> All that glitters is sold as gold.

---

[1] Modern translation by Nevill Coghill, 1951.

ALL TICKETY-BOO

There are many synonymous phrases for this enthusiastic statement that everything is 'fine and dandy'.

'Tickety-boo' may come from the word 'ticket', as in 'that's the ticket'. In the nineteenth century, charities issued tickets to the poor that could be exchanged for soup, clothing and coal.

Other sources suggest that the phrase has its origins with the British Army in India, and that it may be an Anglicized version of the Hindi phrase *tikai babu*, which means 'it's all right, sir'.

ANNUS HORRIBILIS

A particularly bad or miserable year, the phrase being Latin for 'horrible year'. It owes its popularity to Queen Elizabeth II (1926–), who used it in a speech at a banquet in the Guild Hall, London, in 1992 – the year which saw the divorce of the Princess Royal, the separations of the Prince and Princess of Wales and of the Duke and Duchess of York, and the devastating fire at Windsor Castle.

The next day, the punning headline writers had a **field day** (see page 86), with *The Sun* proclaiming on the front page, 'One's Bum Year'.

'Annus horribilis' *was a play on a phrase with the opposite meaning* – annus mirabilis, *which was first used as the title of a poem by John Dryden (1631–1700) to describe the year 1666, which he saw as an example of miraculous intervention by God.*

It has ever since been used to describe particular years full of wonders or achievements; 1759 was one such for the British, in which they achieved a string of military successes (in British naval history, 1759 is also known as the 'Year of Victories').

ANOTHER NAIL IN THE COFFIN

A depressing phrase which is applied to a development that makes a situation progressively worse; one more factor to plunge a person into greater disfavour, to hasten his dismissal,

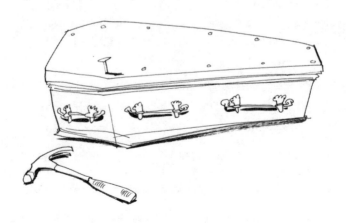

downfall or death. The final nail can be compared with the 'last straw' (see **a drowning man will clutch at a straw**, page 62).

Peter Pindar (Dr J. Wolcot, 1738–1819) wrote in one of his *Expostulary Odes* (1782): 'Care to our coffin adds a nail, no doubt.'

The phrase was also adopted by smokers. As early as the 1920s, they referred to cigarettes as 'coffin nails', and this expression became the stock response whenever someone accepted yet another cigarette.

At the time, they were referring to the hazards of a smoker's cough; the links between smoking, cancer and heart disease were only recognized later (when cigarettes earned another nickname – 'cancer sticks').

APPLE OF ONE'S EYE

'The apple of one's eye' is what one cherishes most. The pupil of the eye has long been referred to as the 'apple' because it is perfectly round and was originally thought to be solid.

Because sight is so precious, someone who was called this as an endearment was similarly precious, with the result that the phrase took on the figurative sense we still retain.

The Bible employs the phrase many times, including:

Keep me as the apple of the eye, hide me under the shadow of thy wings.

Psalms 17:8

The earliest recorded examples of the saying's use in Britain, meanwhile, can be found in the works of King Alfred (849–899), dating from the end of the ninth century.

> Our modern word for the physical 'apple of one's eye', 'pupil', comes from Latin and appeared in English in the sixteenth century. It is figurative in origin; the late Latin original was pupilla, 'little doll'.
>
> The word might have been applied to the dark central portion of the eye within the iris because of the tiny doll-like image of oneself that can be seen when looking into another person's eye.

AS THE ACTRESS SAID TO
THE BISHOP

A rejoinder to a perfectly innocent statement, used to create a sexual double entendre. Typical comments that might encourage such a retort would be, 'I didn't know I had it in me,' or 'I'd bend over backwards to please you.'

The phrase was popular in the 1940s in the RAF, although it is thought to have originated in the music-hall era, when the staple fare of stand-up comedians included many stories of potentially scandalous couplings between bishops and actresses.

In *Educating Archie*, the popular BBC radio show of the 1950s, Beryl Reid as Monica used an alternative version of the phrase: 'As the art mistress said to the gardener.'

TO ASK FOR (OR BE GIVEN)
ONE'S CARDS

To ask for or be given one's cards is to resign from or be dismissed from a job. Used since the 1920s, the phrase originally referred to your employment card, but now means your P45 and other documents kept by one's employer as a record of income tax and insurance contributions.

In a sporting extension of this phrase, if a player, particularly in football, is shown a card by the referee, he is in breach of the rules; a yellow card represents a warning and a red card means the player is sent off the field **to take an early bath** (see page 172).

TO ASK SOMETHING POINT BLANK

To ask a direct question. This is a sixteenth-century phrase from the sport of archery. The targets had a white (*blanc* in French) central spot, so the arrows were pointed at the white, that is *point blanc.*

In military, and especially artillery usage, 'point blank' is a range at which there is no fall of shot due to gravity – in other words, a very close range. (Any projectile from a firearm 'drops' from the point of aim as the range increases, which in turn means that the further the target, the higher the weapon has to be aimed above it.)

AN ASS IN A LION'S SKIN

An old saying to describe a cowardly person who blusters or tries to bully others by acting as if he is better than them; otherwise, a fool with groundless aspirations to wisdom.

The ass or donkey is often used figuratively to symbolize ignorance or stupidity, and this phrase is an allusion to the legendary fable of the ass that dressed in a lion's skin, but betrayed itself by braying.

THE BACK OF BEYOND

This is an Australian expression, nineteenth century in origin, which is now commonly used to describe any remote area, but which originally referred to the vast spaces of the interior of the country, the Great Outback.

The 'back', reduced from 'back country', is the outlying territory behind the settled regions, and the term 'backblock' is found in 1850, referring to those territories of Australia split up by the government into blocks for settlement.

BACK TO SQUARE ONE

To begin again, or, less formally, 'Back to where you started, sunshine!' This colloquialism possibly derives from board games like snakes and ladders, in which players, through bad

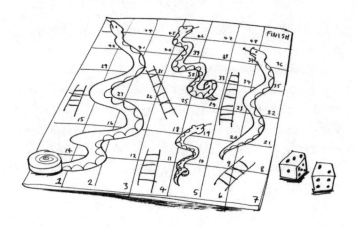

luck or poor judgement, have to move their pieces back to the starting point.

Another suggestion is that it comes from the early days of radio football commentaries, when diagrams of the pitch, divided into numbered squares, were printed in radio listings magazines so that listeners could follow the game.

The expression's meaning is similar to 'Back to the drawing board', which means to go back and rethink a complete project or scheme. Aircraft designers during the Second World War used this phrase when a concept or even a whole design for a new machine proved unworkable and had to be started all over again.

BALLPARK FIGURE

A financial North Americanism that has taken hold in Britain, this is an estimate, or a budget figure, which might better be described as a 'guesstimate'.

A ballpark is a large stadium in America built specifically for the game of baseball, and the phrase 'in the same ballpark' was originally used when two figures, the projected and the real figure, were reasonably close. Over time, the term has evolved so that the estimated figure itself is now known as a 'ballpark figure'.

TO BARK UP THE WRONG TREE

To be totally off the mark, to waste energy following the wrong course of action, or to have one's attention diverted off the subject in hand. The phrase dates back to the 1800s and neatly puns a dog's bark with tree bark.

Its origins stem from the American sport of raccoon hunting. The hounds of the hunting pack are trained to mark the tree in which the raccoon they are pursuing takes shelter, and then to howl at its base until their master arrives to shoot the animal. The hounds may bark up at the wrong tree, however, if the raccoon has managed to evade them.

The expression first became popular in the early nineteenth century, appearing in the works of James Hall (1793–1868), Davy Crockett (1786–1836) – himself a great raccoon hunter – and Albert Pike (1809–91).

BARKING MAD

Used to suggest raving insanity, this phrase is frequently shortened to simply 'barking'. The expression emerged at the beginning of the twentieth century.

Although people often believe it to be associated with the London suburb of Barking – partly because of a lunatic asylum said to have been located there in medieval times – this assumption is inaccurate. In fact, its derivation stems from its rather more obvious link with rabid or mad dogs, whose wild howls and yaps audibly betrayed their diseased state.

TO BEAT ABOUT THE BUSH

To approach a matter indirectly or in a roundabout way.

The expression has evolved from early hunting methods for catching birds. One team of hunters would approach the birds hiding in the undergrowth from the sides, so as to drive them into the path of another team, who would catch them with nets as they took off.

This task of literally beating the bushes in which the birds take shelter is still an important part of pheasant shooting today.

BETWEEN THE DEVIL AND
THE DEEP BLUE SEA

Caught between two evils or dangers, in a dilemma with
nowhere to turn. The saying may be of nautical origin, the
'devil' being a term for a seam in the hull of a ship that ran
along the waterline.

A commonly used modern phrase with a similar meaning is
'between a rock and a hard place'.

*'Between the devil and the deep blue sea' could also have
been inspired by the ancient phrase 'to steer or sail between
Scylla and Charybdis'.*

In Homer's Odyssey, *Scylla was a six-headed monster
who lived in a cavern overlooking a narrow channel off the
coast of Sicily; she seized sailors from every passing ship with
each of her six mouths.*

*On the opposite rock, Charybdis, another monster, lived
under a huge fig tree, from where she sucked in and regorged
the sea, forming a treacherous whirlpool.*

*In the poem, Odysseus sailed between these two perils,
losing his ship in the whirlpool and the crew to Scylla. Only
he survived – by clinging to the fig tree.*

BEWARE GREEKS BEARING GIFTS

Sometimes expressed as 'I fear Greeks even when they offer gifts' (Virgil [70–90 BC], *Aeneid*, 29–19 BC), this saying has its roots in the story of Helen of Troy (see **the face that launched a thousand ships**, page 68) and the Trojan War.

After a ten-year siege of the city of Troy by the Greeks, one of the remaining Greek besiegers (the Odysseus of the previous entry) devised an ingenious plan to invade the city. He hid all his men in a huge wooden horse, which was left outside the city gates, and then the Greeks abandoned their posts. The Trojans mistakenly took the horse to be a tribute from their beaten enemy, and in celebration took the gift to the heart of their stronghold.

When night fell, the Greek soldiers poured out of the horse and – having the element of surprise – were victorious in the final battle.

THE BIG APPLE

The well-known nickname for New York City.

The name was first coined in the 1920s by John J. Fitz Gerald (1893–1963), a reporter for the *Morning Telegraph*, who used it to refer to the city's race tracks and who claimed to have heard it used by black stable hands in New Orleans in 1921.

Black jazz musicians in the 1930s took up the name to refer to the city, especially Harlem, as the jazz capital of the world. The epithet was then revived in 1971 as part of a publicity campaign to attract tourists to New York.

The sentiment behind 'The Big Apple' is likely to be the idea of an apple as a symbol of the best, as in the **apple of one's eye** (see page 17), meaning someone or something that is very precious.

> *In the eighteenth century, the writer and politician Horace Walpole (1717–97) referred to London as 'The Strawberry', being impressed by its freshness and cleanliness compared with foreign cities; he named his estate at Twickenham, Middlesex, Strawberry Hill, and founded there the Strawberry Hill Press.*

THE BIG ENCHILADA

The leader, the top man or woman, the boss.

The phrase crops up in the infamous Watergate tapes, referring to the then US Attorney-General, John Mitchell (1913–88). He led President Nixon's (1913–94) re-election campaign in 1972, and was later indicted on charges that he had conspired to plan the burglary of the Democratic National Committee's headquarters in the Watergate complex in Washington, DC, and had then obstructed justice and perjured himself during the subsequent cover-up; he was convicted in 1974.

'The big enchilada' is a modernized version of earlier phrases that became popular in the mid 1970s, such as 'big gun' or 'the big cheese', both of which are used to describe VIPs, especially in business; a group of them may sometimes be facetiously described as *les grands fromages*.

BIG-STICK DIPLOMACY

A political catchphrase which describes diplomatic negotiations that are backed up by the threat of military force.

The term was brought to public attention in 1901 when then US Vice-President Theodore Roosevelt (1858–1919) revealed in a speech his fondness for the West African proverb 'Speak softly and carry a big stick, you will go far'. (Later, as President, he used such practices successfully in the Alaskan boundary dispute of 1902–4.)

THE BIRDS AND THE BEES

A euphemism for human procreation which was probably inspired by songwriter Cole Porter (1891–1964), thanks to his 1954 composition, 'Let's Do It':

> Birds do it, bees do it,
> Even educated fleas do it,
> Let's do it, let's fall in love.

The phrase was used, often by embarrassed parents or teachers, as a means of avoiding dangerous words like 'sex' or 'sexual intercourse'; nowadays, it tends to be used ironically.

BISH-BASH-BOSH

A yuppie phrase, coined in the 1980s, to describe something done well, quickly and efficiently. It was later shortened to 'bosh' and widely used by manual workers, as if to say 'just like that' or 'sorted'.

It gained mass circulation in the 1990s thanks to the comedian Harry Enfield (1961–), who made it the catchphrase of one of his characters, a loutish but high-earning plasterer called 'Loadsamoney'.

> *'Yuppie' is another phrase that emerged in the 1980s; it was originally a twisted acronym of 'young urban professional'. It is still used today to describe well-paid middle-class workers who are 'on the up' in their careers, and is often applied to those employed in the City.*

TO BITE THE BULLET

To undertake the most challenging part of a feat of endurance, to face danger with courage and fortitude, to behave stoically or to knuckle down to some difficult or unpleasant task.

The expression originated in field surgery before the use of anaesthetics. A surgeon about to operate on a wounded soldier would give him a bullet to bite on, both to distract him from the pain and to make him less likely to cry out.

TO BITE THE DUST

To fall down dead. The Scottish author Tobias Smollett (1721–71) was the first to put this expression in print in 1750, in his translation of Alain-René Le Sage's (1668–1747) *Adventures of Gil Blas of Santillane*; while in Samuel Butler's (1835–1902) 1898 translation of Homer's *The Iliad* Achilles has the line:

> Grant that my sword may pierce the shirt of Hector about his heart, and that full many of his comrades may bite the dust as they fall dying round him.

Another version of the phrase – 'lick the dust' – had the same meaning and appeared in the original (1611) edition of the King James Bible.

The phrase was in common use during the Second World War, especially in the RAF; today, it is more often used to describe the failure of an idea, plan or task than death or injury.

TO THE BITTER END

To the last extremity, to the final defeat, or to the death. An affliction can be borne until the bitter end, meaning to the last stroke of bad fortune.

'Bitter end' is a mid-nineteenth-century nautical term for the end of a rope or chain secured in a vessel's chain locker. When there is no windlass (winch), such cables are fastened to bitts –

that is, pairs of bollards fixed to the deck – and when the rope is let out until no more remains, the end is at the bitts: hence the 'bitter end'.

However, the phrase appears in the Old Testament in the context that we use today, and some etymologists believe that this is the true source of the expression:

> Her end is bitter as wormwood, sharp as a two-edged sword.
> Proverbs 5:4

THE BLACK DOG

The metaphorical 'black dog' has various personalities. Horace wrote that to see a black dog with its pups was a bad omen, and the Devil has frequently been symbolized by a black dog.

After British Prime Minister Winston Churchill (1874–1965) referred to his depression as his 'black dog', the phrase also became a metaphor for this specific form of mental illness.

In addition, 'black dog' is eighteenth-century slang for a counterfeit silver coin made of washed pewter. Even then, 'black' when applied to ill-begotten money was a familiar term.

There is another phrase, 'to blush like a black dog', which means not to blush at all.

BLOOD, SWEAT AND TEARS

An emphatic description of the effort required to complete a challenging task. It is a concise form of a phrase used by Winston Churchill in his first speech to the House of Commons upon taking over as Prime Minister, on 13 May 1940.

Yet Churchill may have been inspired by a number of sources; some three centuries earlier, John Donne (*c.* 1572–1631) wrote in 'An Anatomy of the World' (1611), 'Mollify it with thy tears, or sweat, or blood'; while Lord Byron (1788–1824) observed in *The Age of Bronze* (1823):

> Year after year they voted cent per cent,
> Blood, sweat and tear wrung millions – why? For the rent!

At the time of Churchill's assumption of the highest political office, British morale was at a low ebb: Nazi forces had overrun Denmark, Holland and Belgium, and were in the process of conquering Norway and France. The prospect of victory over Germany looked increasingly unlikely.

Churchill's actual words were, 'I have nothing to offer but blood, toil, tears and sweat,' and he revisited this phrase several times during the war years.

TO BLOW THE GAFF

A slang phrase meaning to reveal a secret, which may derive from the French *gaffe*, a blunder, but is more likely to come from 'gab', the informal English word for 'speech', which in turn derives from 'gob', meaning 'mouth' or 'beak' (the expression 'gift of the gab' comes from the same source).

Current in the eighteenth century was the slang expression 'to blow the gab', meaning to betray a secret.

'Gaff' is also archaic English slang for someone's home, as in: 'Let's go round to his gaff.'

A more colourful derivation may be that 'to blow the gaff' refers to the exposure of a concealed device, known as a gaff, used to cheat at cards. This was a small hook set in a ring worn on the finger, which was used by the crooked player to grip the cards.

TO BLOW HOT AND COLD

To be inconsistent, to have fluctuating opinions, or simply to be unable to make up one's mind.

The expression has its origins in the Aesop's fable that describes the experience of a traveller who accepted the hospitality of a satyr (one of the gods of the forest, a creature who is part goat and part man).

The chilly traveller blew on his cold fingers to warm them – and then blew on his hot broth to cool it. The indignant satyr ejected him because he blew both hot and cold with the same breath.

TO BONE UP ON

To study intensively, to engage in serious research into a particular subject, or to revise a subject comprehensively.

Some sources suggest that the phrase is an allusion to whalebone in a corset, which sculpts the shape and stiffens the garment, as a metaphor for the gaining of 'hard knowledge'.

Others believe it came from the Victorian practice of using bone to polish leather, and that it indicated a polishing or refinement of knowledge.

However, in the nineteenth century a publishing firm owned by Henry Bohn (1796–1884) produced English translations of Greek and Latin classics that were widely used by students cramming for their exams – and it is possible that the expression 'to Bohn up' may have evolved into 'bone up'.

TO BE BORN ON THE WRONG SIDE OF THE TRACKS

To be born on the wrong side of the tracks is a disadvantage, as it was the part of town deemed to be both socially and environmentally inferior.

The expression originated in America, where railway lines ran through the centre of towns. Poor and industrial areas were often located to one side of the railroad tracks because the prevailing wind would blow smoke from the railway and smog in that direction, leaving the better-off neighbourhoods unpolluted.

The phrase is now used to refer to anyone who comes from a poor or rough background.

THE BOTTOM LINE

The main point of an argument, the basic characteristic of something, the actual value of a financial deal, or the nub or truth of the matter.

The phrase itself is an accounting term, and refers to the figure at the end of a financial statement, indicating the net profit or loss of a company.

'The bottom line' gained wide currency as a phrase during the 1970s, possibly because of its frequent use by the US Secretary of State, Henry Kissinger (1923–). He spoke of 'the bottom line' as the eventual outcome of a negotiation – ignoring the distraction of any inessential detail.

BREAK A LEG!

The theatre is notoriously superstitious, and among actors it is deemed bad luck to wish a colleague 'good luck' before going on stage. Instead, this phrase – a traditional, if somewhat black, euphemism – is employed to wish someone luck in a performance, especially on opening night.

There are a number of possible sources for the expression and the earliest recorded use is in fact German; Luftwaffe pilots in the Second World War would send each other off to fight with the cheery saying '*Hals und Beinbruch*', meaning 'break your neck and leg'.

The phrase was also used in English around this time to mean 'make a strenuous effort', so it may have simply been an instruction to put on the best show you possibly could.

A more fanciful explanation is that the saying came from the assassination of President Abraham Lincoln (1809–65) in his private box at Ford's Theatre, Washington, DC, on 14 April 1865.

The murderer, John Wilkes Booth (1838–65), a reputable Shakespearean actor, escaped after firing the shot by leaping down on to the stage, breaking his leg in the process.

BRIGHT YOUNG THINGS

A phrase coined by the tabloid press in the late 1920s to describe the hedonistic young socialites who partied their way through the years following the First World War.

As a counterpoint to the horrors of war, it was all the rage to dance the night away in a riot of frivolous partying, possibly in a subconscious attempt to deny that the war had ever happened, or at least to try to forget the bloody conflict.

The phrase is now used to describe each successive generation of young, fashionable people.

In 2003, Stephen Fry (1957–) directed a movie called Bright Young Things, *which was based on the Evelyn Waugh (1903–66) novel* Vile Bodies *(1930).*

THE BUCK STOPS HERE

A declaration meaning 'this is where ultimate responsibility lies'.

The most likely origin for the phrase is the poker table, where a buckhorn knife was placed before the player whose turn it was to deal. 'Passing the buck' meant passing responsibility on to the next player.

> *The phrase was made famous by US President Harry S. Truman (1884–1972; president 1945–53), who had it handwritten on a sign on his desk at the White House to remind himself and those around him that he alone had the ultimate responsibility for every decision of his administration.*
>
> *Some twenty-five years later, President Jimmy Carter (1924–) had the legend reinstated with the same idea in mind.*

BUSINESS AS USUAL

This self-explanatory expression was widely used in Britain in the Second World War, and especially during the London Blitz and the blitzes on other major cities, when shops and businesses continued to open in spite of bomb damage. In the capital, 'Business as usual' and 'London can take it' were commonly scrawled defiantly on the walls of damaged buildings.

Winston Churchill popularized the phrase in 1941 in a speech at the Guild Hall in London when he said, 'The maxim of the British people is: "Business as usual."'

> *A later Conservative Prime Minister, Margaret (now Baroness) Thatcher (1925–) memorably evoked the fighting spirit behind these words after the lethal IRA bomb attack on the Grand Hotel in Brighton, in which she was lucky to escape death or serious injury, during the Conservative Party Conference of 1984.*

BY A LONG CHALK

This is a sporting expression and means to win easily, far ahead of the competition. Before lead pencils became common, merit marks or scores used to be made with chalk: in a game of skittles or darts, for example, individual points were referred to as a 'chalk'; a long chalk, therefore, is a high score.

BY THE SKIN OF ONE'S TEETH

By the narrowest margin. There are several metaphors with the meaning 'only just' and many allude to body parts (for example, 'by a hair's breadth'), emphasizing the physical danger of a given situation from which one might have just escaped.

'By the skin of one's teeth' specifically is a (slightly misquoted) biblical phrase that means to have suffered 'a close shave':

> My bone cleaveth to my skin, and to my flesh, and I am escaped with the skin of my teeth.
>
> Job 19:20

TO CALL OFF ALL BETS

A summons to cancel all wagers, deriving from the race track and the betting shop; for instance, a bookmaker may call off all bets if he suspects that a race or other contest has been rigged.

In a widening of its meaning, the phrase is used to mean rejecting a complicated or disadvantageous issue.

In African-American slang of the 1940s, however, it meant 'to die' – indeed, the most final way of calling off all bets.

TO CARRY A TORCH

To suffer unrequited love. Since the late 1920s, this phrase has been used to describe a long-standing emotional attachment that is either undeclared or not returned.

The torch represents the flame of undying love, and this symbolism may come from depictions of Venus, the goddess of love, holding a burning torch. •

> *A 'torch singer' is (usually) a female who sings sentimental love songs. It is thought that the expression 'torch song', in this sense, may have been coined by Broadway nightclub singer Tommy Lyman in the 1930s.*

TO CASE THE JOINT

An American slang expression from the criminal fraternity meaning to inspect or reconnoitre a building before attempting to rob it or break into it for some other nefarious purpose.

'Joint' in this context means 'a building': an early twentieth-century colloquial Americanism for a sleazy dive where opium could be smoked or, during the Prohibition era (1920–33), where illicit spirits could be bought and drunk. The word 'joint' has since come to be generally applied disparagingly to almost any disreputable establishment.

TO CAST THE FIRST STONE

To be first to criticize, to find fault, to start a quarrel, or to cast aspersions on someone's character. In biblical times, the barbaric custom of capital punishment was to pelt heretics, adulteresses and criminals with stones and rocks in a public place.

The phrase is from John 8:7, spoken by Jesus to the Scribes and Pharisees who brought before him a woman caught in adultery. They said that according to the law of Moses, she should be stoned to death, to which Jesus replied: 'He that is without sin among you, let him first cast a stone at her.'

TO CAST PEARLS BEFORE SWINE

To offer something precious or of quality to someone who is perceived to be too ignorant or uncultured to understand or appreciate it. To show, for example, a brilliant idea or a work of art to an unappreciative audience or to the kind of person known as a Philistine.

(Philistines were warlike immigrants to Philistia in ancient Palestine, who fought the Israelites for possession of the land, and came to be stigmatized as an uneducated, heathen enemy; the term has since by extension come to mean anyone unreceptive or hostile to culture, especially someone who is smugly and boorishly so.)

The phrase itself comes from the New Testament (Matthew 7:6): 'Give not that which is holy unto the dogs, neither cast ye your pearls before swine, lest they trample them under their feet.'

CAT GOT YOUR TONGUE?

A question directed at a silent partner in a conversation to ask why they're not speaking.

The earliest written example appeared in 1911, according to the *Oxford English Dictionary*, but it may have been around since the mid nineteenth century.

As to its origins, numerous theories abound; none firmly proved. Some argue that it must stem from ancient Middle Eastern punishment techniques, when liars' tongues were ripped out and then fed to kings' cats; while others cite the much-feared whip the 'cat-o'-nine-tails' as the source of the phrase, insinuating that this nasty weapon, used to flog sailors, forced them into silence – both through fear and pain.

THE CAT'S PYJAMAS

This colloquialism first surfaced in America in the 1920s to describe something or someone superlatively good or top-notch, and has retained its meaning for almost a hundred years.

Alternative sources suggest that the phrase may come from an early nineteenth-century English tailor E. B. Katz, who apparently made the finest silk pyjamas, though there is scant evidence to prove this is true.

'The cat's whiskers' and *'the bee's knees'* are phrases with similar meaning. In the 1920s, people played with phrases that linked animals to humans, and so we find *'the kipper's knickers'*, *'the snake's hips'*, *'the elephant's instep'* and so on.

In the last twenty years, modern imagination has taken this idea further, and we now have more ribald phrases such as *'the dog's bollocks' (which is sometimes abbreviated to just 'the dog's').*

CATCH-22

A Catch-22 situation is a lose-lose situation; whichever alternative you choose, you can't win.

It is the title of Joseph Heller's (1923–99) highly regarded satirical novel published in 1955. The story centres on Captain Yossarian of the 256th US Army Air Force bombing squadron in the Second World War, whose main aim in life is to avoid being killed. The best way for a pilot to achieve this was to be grounded due to insanity …

There was only one catch and that was Catch-22, which specified that concern for one's own safety in the face of dangers that were real and immediate was the process of a rational mind. Orr [another pilot] was crazy and could be grounded. All he had to do was to ask and as soon as he did, he would no longer be crazy and would have to fly more missions.

CHARLIE'S DEAD

A slang euphemism used to indicate that a woman's petticoat is showing below the hem of her skirt. The phrase was a useful way for ladies to convey to one another that their petticoats were hanging low, without having to state something so indelicate in front of any men present.

The expression has two possible sources, both involving kings. One is the execution of Charles I (1600–49) on 30 January 1649, at which the women in attendance are said to have dipped their petticoats in his blood as a way of honouring him.

The other possibility is that it refers to the habit of flirtatious female fans of the dashing Charles II (1630–85): they would flash the hems of their petticoats to show how much they admired him.

TO CLAM UP

To refuse to talk, to stop talking, to become silent. People are generally said to 'clam up' when they are trying to defend themselves.

The phrase takes its origins from the closed shell of a live clam. At high tide, clams open their shells a little to allow seawater to filter through, so that they can feed. When the tide goes out, they close their shells tightly to retain the water and protect themselves from predators.

CLEAN ROUND THE BEND

Completely crazy or eccentric. The phrase was described by F. C. Bowen in the *Oxford English Dictionary* in 1929 as 'an old naval term for anybody who is mad'.

In a neat play on words, the phrase has been used to advertise the lavatory cleaner Harpic since the 1930s: 'It cleans right round the bend.'

> *The word 'clean' is used in many different ways to describe something complete, pure, unmarked or unreserved – for instance, 'clean bowled', 'to make a clean break' or 'to make a clean breast of it'.*

TO CLEAR THE DECKS

To remove everything not required, especially when preparing for action; hence, to prepare for some task by removing the extraneous or irrelevant.

This is a nautical phrase and alludes to a sailing ship preparing for battle, when anything in the way of the guns and their crews, or that might burn or splinter, or that was not lashed down, was removed from the usually cluttered decks so that no untethered articles would roll about and injure the seamen during the battle.

This saying is used in many contexts, such as clearing the table of food and dishes, or preparing the house to receive guests.

TO BE IN A CLEFT STICK

A figurative phrase meaning to be in a tight place or dilemma with no room for manoeuvre, neither backwards nor forwards.

The expression may come from the verb 'to cleave', which has two directly opposite meanings: one being to stick to or adhere, and the other to split, chop or break along a grain or line of cleavage.

The first recorded use of the phrase with its figurative meaning was by the poet William Cowper (1731–1800) in 1782: 'We are squeezed to death, between the two sides of that sort of alternative which is commonly called a cleft stick.'

A cleft stick was often used in the eighteenth century to catch snakes. The form of torture inflicted on Ariel by the witch Sycorax in Shakespeare's The Tempest *(1611) was to imprison him in the trunk of a cleft pine tree.*

TO CLIMB ON THE BANDWAGON

To declare support for a popular movement or trend, usually without believing in the movement or trend.

The expression is believed to have originated in the Southern states of America, probably dating from the first presidential campaign of William Jennings Bryan (1860–1925) in 1892, when candidates for political office would parade through the streets, led by a band of musicians performing on a large horse-drawn dray.

As a publicity stunt, the local candidate would mount the wagon as it passed and ride through his constituency in an attempt to gain personal support from the voters. Perhaps unsurprisingly, Bryan never won the presidency, losing to McKinley in 1896 and 1900, and to Taft in 1908.

CLOAK AND DAGGER

Any operation that involves some intrigue, especially the melodramatic undercover activities of those involved in espionage or other secret work.

Cloak-and-dagger plays were swashbuckling adventures popular in the seventeenth century. In France, a performance of this type was known as a *comédie de cape et d'épée* and this is the direct source of the English phrase, 'cloak and dagger'.

The name also appears in the Spanish comedias de capa y espada, *literally 'comedies of cloak and sword', particularly those by the Spanish dramatists Lope de Vega (1562–1635) and Calderón (1600–81), although their plays were dramas of merely domestic intrigue.*

ON CLOUD NINE

To be on cloud nine means to be in a state of elation, very happy indeed, or feeling 'as high as a kite'.

This fanciful twentieth-century expression comes from the terminology used by the United States Weather Bureau. The Bureau divides clouds into classes, and each class into nine types.

Cloud nine is cumulonimbus, a cumulus cloud that develops to a vast height, with rounded masses of white vapour heaped one on the other; the upper parts resembling the shapes of domes, mountains or towers, while the base is practically horizontal.

COCK-AND-BULL STORY

A rambling or incredible tale; a tall story invented as an excuse; a lie.

There are various possible explanations for the derivation of this term. In the coaching days of the seventeenth century, the London coach changed horses at the Bull Inn and the Birmingham coach at the Cock Inn. The waiting passengers of both coaches would exchange stories and jokes. The 'Cock-and-Bull' story is said to have originated from this scenario.

The phrase may derive, however, from ancient fables in which cocks and bulls and other animals conversed. In his Boyle Lecture of 1692, Richard Bentley (1662–1742) stated:

> That cocks and bulls might discourse, and hinds and panthers hold conferences about religion.

While in his novel *Tristram Shandy* (1759), Laurence Sterne (1713–68) wrote:

> 'L—d!' said my mother. 'What is all this story about?'
> 'A Cock and Bull,' said Yorick – 'And one of the best of its kind, I have ever heard.'

Today, both words are commonly employed separately in a slang or vulgar context. 'Bull' is used as in 'what a load of bull', politely avoiding saying the word 'bullshit', while 'cock' speaks for itself.

A Scottish satire or lampooning story is known as a 'cockalane', which is taken directly from the French phrase of the same meaning as 'cock and bull': coq et l'âne (cock and ass, donkey or fool).

COLD ENOUGH TO FREEZE THE BALLS OFF A BRASS MONKEY

This means that the weather is extremely cold, and although the expression sounds delightfully vulgar, it was not in fact originally a reference to monkeys' testicles.

A brass monkey is a type of rack in which cannon balls were stored. Being brass, the 'monkey' contracted in cold weather, resulting in the cannonballs being ejected.

The expression has also mutated to a shortened form, again a comment on the temperature, as 'brass-monkey weather'.

TO COME A CROPPER

To fall heavily, head over heels, or to fail ignominiously.

The origin probably lies in the old term for the hindquarters of a horse, the croup or crupper. If you fell from a horse in the eighteenth century, you were said to have fallen neck and crop, which came to be used colloquially to mean headlong or head over heels. So to fall to the ground neck and crop is to 'come a cropper'.

We now use the phrase to mean 'to get into trouble' or 'to fail', rather than literally 'to fall'.

TO COME OUT OF THE CLOSET

To declare one's homosexuality, to come out into the open about it. The term was used by the American gay rights organization the Gay Liberation Front from about 1969, but the idea of 'coming out' had first been encouraged by German gay-rights advocate Karl Heinrich Ulrichs (1825–95) in 1869.

In the days when homosexuality was a criminal offence, gay men had to hide the nature of their sexual preferences. (Lesbianism had never been criminalized in Britain, since at the time the legislation was formulated, Queen Victoria, 1819–1901, refused to believe that sexual relations between women could ever occur.) They became known as closet queens, the closet being a private room.

When anti-homosexual laws were repealed, the need for secrecy receded and gay men were able 'to come out' –

although many, fearful of society's disapproval, remained 'in the closet'.

The expression is now often used generally to mean 'to declare one's real position'.

> *The phrase 'to come out' was used in the first half of the twentieth century to describe debutantes, upper-class young women who were presented at Court during the Season, so making their official debut in society.*

TO COME UP TO SCRATCH

To be good enough to pass a test; to make the grade. This is a colloquialism from the boxing ring dating back to the nineteenth century.

Under the London Prize Ring Rules introduced in 1839, a round in a prizefight ended when one of the fighters was knocked down. After an interval of thirty seconds, the floored fighter was given eight seconds to make his way, unaided, to a mark scratched in the centre of the ring.

If he failed to reach the mark, he had not 'come up to scratch' and was declared the loser of the bout.

COUCH POTATO

American slang from the late 1980s, used to describe a 'telly addict', someone who indulges in the habit of lounging at home watching television, eating and drinking, but never taking exercise.

The expression is now used in most English-speaking countries, particularly with the increase in the number of television channels to choose from.

Perhaps the potato featured in the metaphor because the blemishes on its skin are known as 'eyes'; or possibly because it is the tuber of the potato plant, thus punning with 'the tube' – the television.

TO COVER ONE'S ASS

A slang term, American in origin, meaning to make up an excuse or prepare an alibi in advance, in order to avoid being blamed if something goes wrong.

The phrase originated in the 1960s among US troops in Vietnam, stemming from the military phrase 'to cover one's rear', as in defend yourself from a possible attack from behind, and later became part of colloquial American language.

It came to Britain in the 1980s, and is commonly used today in the planning of business ventures – or in contracts, in which 'ass-covering clauses' are frequently included as a means of safeguarding the signatory against the unexpected, and thus blame.

TO CROSS THE RUBICON

To take an irrevocable step, to burn one's bridges, to go beyond the point of no return.

The Rubicon was a small river, possibly the present-day Fiumicino, which formed the border between ancient Italy and Cisalpine Gaul, the province allocated to Julius Caesar (100–44 BC). When Caesar crossed this stream in 49 BC, he went beyond the limits of his own province and thus became an invader in Italy, making the outbreak of war between Pompey (106–48 BC) and the Senate inevitable.

'The Rubicon' is now often used alone as a description of 'the point of no return'.

TO CRY ALL THE WAY TO THE BANK

The expression 'to cry all the way to the bank' was a popular catchphrase in the 1950s. It is an ironic comment, usually made about someone who has done something questionable, or produced something kitsch or tasteless or for some reason generally disapproved of, while making a great deal of money from it.

It is thought to have been first used by the high-camp pianist and entertainer Liberace (1919–87) in 1956, after critics had savaged his performance at a Madison Square Gardens concert. Liberace was the highest-paid entertainer in the United States during the 1960s and 1970s, and his income averaged $5 million a year for more than twenty-five years.

THE CURATE'S EGG

'Good in parts, like the curate's egg' has become something of a proverb.

The curate's egg first appeared in a cartoon published in the satirical magazine *Punch* in 1895. It showed a timid young curate at his bishop's breakfast table, too nervous to say that his egg is bad.

Right Reverend Host: I'm afraid you've got a bad egg, Mr Jones.
Curate: Oh, no, my Lord, I assure you! Parts of it are excellent!

The phrase was originally used to refer to something bad that is said to be good out of politeness, though in modern use it has evolved to describe something that is part good, part bad.

TO CUT THE MUSTARD

A zesty and confident phrase meaning to do something well and efficiently, to prove oneself beyond all expectations at completing a task or occupation.

The expression probably derives from mustard as slang for 'the best'; a line from O. Henry's (1862–1910) *Cabbages and Kings* (1894) reads:

I'm not headlined in the bills, but I'm the mustard in the salad just the same.

'To cut', in this phrase, might refer to the harvesting of the plant, but it also might be used as in the expressions to 'cut a dash', 'cut up rough' or 'cut capers'.

TO CUT YOUR COAT ACCORDING TO YOUR CLOTH

This metaphorical proverb dates back to the sixteenth century and is all about good housekeeping and living within one's means. It is self-evidently sensible advice to keep to one's budget and restrict expenditure to the amount of one's income.

It is often shortened, becoming simply 'to cut your coat'.

DEAR-JOHN LETTER

A 'you're dumped' note from a wife or girlfriend breaking the news that the relationship with the recipient is over.

The expression originated during the Second World War and is thought to be American. The unfortunate objects of Dear-John letters were usually members of the armed forces overseas, whose female partners at home had made new liaisons, proving that absence sometimes did not make the heart grow fonder.

The name 'John' was often used to signify 'everyman' at the time; 'John Doe' was the name given to any man whose real name was unknown or had to be kept anonymous, like our 'Joe Bloggs' today.

A DOG IN A MANGER

A mean-spirited person who will not let others use something that he has no use for himself.

The phrase comes from a fable attributed to Aesop written in about 600 BC, of a dog that made his bed in a manger of hay. When an ox disturbed him, he snarled and drove the ox away. He would not allow the ox to come near to eat the hay, despite the fact that he could not eat it himself.

The ox leaves the stable muttering the moral of the tale: 'Ah, people often grudge others what they cannot enjoy themselves.'

THE DOG DAYS OF SUMMER

Very hot and oppressive summer days. The Romans called the hottest weeks of the summer *caniculares dies*, and not because dogs are thought to go mad in the heat (although Noël Coward [1899–1973] did write in 1932 that 'mad dogs and Englishmen go out in the midday sun').

The theory was that the days when the Dog Star, Sirius – the brightest star in the firmament – rose with the sun were the hottest and most sultry. It is an ancient belief that the combined heat of Sirius and the sun produced the stifling weather from about 3 July to 11 August.

We also now use the phrase 'dog days' to describe any period of stagnation.

DON'T COUNT YOUR CHICKENS UNTIL THEY ARE HATCHED

Don't assume something is certain before it is proved to be so. The phrase has been around for thousands of years, since it appears in Aesop's fable of 'The Milkmaid and Her Pail'.

There are probably more versions of this proverb than any other. 'The man that once did sell the lion's skin / While the beast liv'd, was kill'd with hunting him,' wrote Shakespeare in Henry V *(1598–9; 4:3), while a Hindu proverb urges, 'Don't bargain for fish which are still in the water,' and an ancient Egyptian saw cautions, 'Do not rejoice over what has not yet happened.'*

DON'T LOOK A GIFT HORSE IN THE MOUTH

(see also **straight from the horse's mouth**, page 168)

This references the method of assessing the age of a horse by inspecting the length of its teeth. The meaning is: do not question the value of something given to you. It is very bad form to inspect a gift for faults or defects, so be grateful for anything received. As the old saying goes: 'It's the thought that counts.'

The phrase is an old proverb that has been in use for hundreds of years. It was discovered in the writings of St Jerome, one of the Latin Fathers of the fourth century, who identified it as a common proverb. The saying also occurs in French, German, Italian, Spanish and other European languages, emphasizing the centuries-long dominance of the horse until the coming of the motor car.

AT THE DROP OF A HAT

On signal, instantly, without delay.

The expression alludes to the American frontier practice of dropping a hat as a signal for a boxing or wrestling match to begin, usually the only formality observed. Athletics or horse races also used to be started by the fast downward sweep of a hat.

There are many sayings including the word 'hat', such as 'hats off to him', 'as black as your hat', and 'I'll eat my hat', all of which probably originated in the days when dress codes and social etiquette were more formal, requiring people in polite society to cover their heads.

A DROWNING MAN WILL CLUTCH AT A STRAW

Someone in desperate circumstances will reach out and grab hold of anything, however flimsy or inadequate, in the hope of surviving the situation. The phrase is often shortened to 'clutching at straws'.

It was first used in print by Sir Thomas More (1478–1535) in 1534, in his *Dialogue of Comfort Against Tribulation*.

> *The word 'straw' has been used as a metaphor for years, representing the insubstantial or groundless, as in a 'man of straw', someone financially insecure or with a poor credit rating. We also have 'the last straw (that broke the camel's back)', that little extra burden which makes something no longer bearable (as with the camel's load, tipping the balance of tolerance).*

AS DRUNK AS A LORD

This simile must have first become common in the eighteenth century, when the consumption of alcohol was something well-bred gentlemen liked to boast about.

At that time, people from the lower social classes simply could not afford to buy the amount of alcohol required to get one very drunk. Consequently, excessive consumption became a clear sign of wealth.

AS EASY AS PIE

Making a pie is not easy and this expression must apply to the eating of it. It originates in nineteenth-century America, where sweet pie was a common dish and the word 'pie' was associated with simple pleasures.

An easy task can also be described as a 'piece of cake', which is also easy to obtain and eat, as opposed to baking it.

TO EAT HUMBLE PIE

To make a humble apology or to submit oneself to a certain degree of humiliation, to climb down from a position one has assumed, to be obliged to take a lower station.

Here, 'humble' could be a play on the word 'umble', the umbles being the offal – the heart, liver and entrails – of an animal, usually the deer, considered a delicacy by some, although most thought them only fit for the servants.

Though the word humble has a different derivation, the closeness of the two words could be one of the reasons the phrase evolved as it did. For when the lord of the manor and his family dined on venison at high table, the huntsman and lower orders of the household took lower seats and partook of the umbles made into a pie.

James Russell Lowell (1819–91) observed in 1864:

Disguise it as you will, flavour it as you will, call it what you will, umble pie is umble pie, and nothing else.

AT THE ELEVENTH HOUR

Just in the nick of time, at the last moment, before the end of the day.

The allusion is to Jesus's parable of the labourers hired to work in the vineyard in which those starting work at the eleventh hour – that is, late in the afternoon at about five o'clock – were paid the same as those who had 'borne the burden and heat of the day' (Matthew 20:1–16).

> *The Allies' armistice with Germany, ending the First World War, came into effect at the eleventh hour of the eleventh day of the eleventh month in 1918.*

THE ENGLISH DISEASE

The poor old English have been blamed for many complaints and *malaises* over the years. Since Columbus's time, the French have described syphilis as the English disease; the English retort to this insult was to call it the French disease.

Later, after the Industrial Revolution, the damp English climate combined with sooty smog meant that bronchitis was prevalent, and it became known as the English disease all over the world.

Now some social ailments tend to be described as English, including class differences, poor industrial relations and economic stagnation. In the 1950s and 1960s, when England was under the sway of the all-powerful trade unions, industrial strikes were widely known as the English disease.

More recently, football hooliganism, both at home and abroad, has been dubbed the English disease.

EVERY CLOUD HAS A SILVER LINING

In every situation, no matter how seemingly hopeless and gloomy, there is always some redeeming brightness to be found if one takes the trouble to look for it – 'while there's life, there's hope.'

This optimistic guidance to look on the bright side has been around since Roman times (although one Latin proverb reads, 'After the sun, the clouds').

The phrase is thought to have its origins in Milton's (1608–74) *Comus* (1634): the lady lost in the wood resolves not to give up hope and says:

Was I deceived or did a sable cloud
Turn forth her silver lining on the night?

EVERY DOG HAS ITS DAY

This is a commonly used phrase that seems to have first appeared in English in the writings of R. Taverner in 1539 and subsequently in those of Shakespeare:

Let Hercules himself do what he may,
The cat will mew, and dog will have his day.

Hamlet (1600; 5:1)

It means that everyone will have a chance one day; everyone will have a moment of success or of being important eventually. This sentiment has been expressed for thousands of years.

> *The Latin proverb reads* Hodie mihi – cras tibi, *'Today to me, tomorrow to thee.' And another ancient old wives' tale states that: 'Fortune visits every man once, she favours me now, but she will favour you in your turn.'*
>
> *As a further example, Peter Pindar wrote in his* Odes to Condolence *(1792):*
>
> *Thus every dog at last will have his day –*
> *He who this morning smiled, at night may sorrow,*
> *The grub today's a butterfly tomorrow.*

AN EYE FOR AN EYE

Punishment equal to the crime, retaliation in kind, or simply getting even. The justification for this form of retribution comes from the Old Testament:

> Eye for eye, tooth for tooth, hand for hand, foot for foot.
>
> Exodus 21:24

Jesus referred to these words in the New Testament and put his own spin on their message, creating another commonly used expression, 'to turn the other cheek':

> Ye have heard that it hath been said, An eye for an eye, and a tooth for a tooth: But I say unto you, That ye resist not evil: but whosoever shall smite thee on thy right cheek, turn to him the other also.
>
> Matthew 5:38–9

THE FACE THAT LAUNCHED A THOUSAND SHIPS

The face is that of the legendary beauty, Helen of Troy, and the ships were the Greek fleet, which sailed for Troy to avenge the King of Sparta.

In Greek legend, Helen was the daughter of Zeus and Leda, and wife of Menelaus, King of Sparta. She eloped with Paris, Prince of Troy, and the angry Menelaus sent a thousand ships to lay siege to the city of Troy. The fabled Helen is now an archetype of female beauty.

The phrase itself was first written by Christopher Marlowe (1564–93):

Was this the face that launched a thousand ships,
And burned the topless towers of Ilium?

Doctor Faustus (first published 1604)

TO BE FAMOUS FOR FIFTEEN MINUTES

Meaning to have short-lived fame, of the type that is now quite possible in the modern, media-driven, celebrity-obsessed age.

The expression comes from the celebrated words of Andy Warhol (1928–87), first published in a catalogue for an exhibition of his work in Stockholm in 1968. Pop artist Warhol was concerned, amongst other subjects, with the nature of celebrity, and he wrote, 'In the future, everyone will be world famous for fifteen minutes.'

The phrase struck a chord and is often now shortened to 'he's had his fifteen minutes'.

A FEATHER IN ONE'S CAP

A personal achievement or honour to be proud of. The feather is a proud and visible emblem of victory and the gesture of putting a feather in your hat is almost universal in one form or another.

There is an ancient custom, widespread in Asia, among Native Americans *and* throughout Europe, of adding a feather to one's headgear to mark each enemy killed. Even today, a sportsman who kills his first woodcock puts a feather from the bird in his hat.

At one time in Hungary, the only people who could wear feathers were those who had killed Turks.

When General Charles Gordon (1833–85), known as 'Chinese Gordon', quelled the Taiping Rebellion in 1864, he was honoured by the Chinese government with the 'yellow jacket and peacock's feather'.

TO FIDDLE WHILE ROME BURNS

To delay or vacillate or do nothing during an emergency or crisis – an allusion to Nero's reputed behaviour during the burning of Rome in AD 64.

Nero Claudius Caesar (AD 37–68) was the infamous Roman emperor whom his contemporaries believed to be the instigator of the fire that destroyed most of the city. As the blaze raged, it is said that he sang to his lyre and recited his own poetry, whilst enjoying the spectacle from the top of a high tower.

Many historians doubt his complicity, however, and Nero himself blamed the Christians.

TO FIGHT LIKE KILKENNY CATS

This is a fight to the end, no holds (as in wrestling) barred.

The connection between fighting and Kilkenny cats is obscure. From the Norman period until 1843, the city of Kilkenny was divided into Englishtown and Irishtown, with much strife between the two. One theory harks back to a legendary battle between a thousand cats from Kilkenny and a thousand cats from other parts of Ireland. In the night-long battle, all the Kilkenny cats survived victorious, while all the others perished.

Another, more popular, theory dates from about 1800, when Kilkenny was occupied by a group of Hessian mercenaries in British government service, some of whom, bored and with nothing better to do, tied two cats to a clothes line by their tails and sat back to enjoy the feline fight.

However, when an officer approached to investigate the noise, the soldiers had no time to release the cats, so they cut the animals free by severing their tails. The officer was told that the cats had fought so fiercely, only their tails remained.

TO BE IN FINE FETTLE

To be in good order or condition – 'fettle' is an old word meaning condition, order or shape. Nowadays, it rarely appears on its own, being usually heard in the alliterative phrase.

In the past, we might have heard 'good fettle' or 'bad fettle', and in *John Barleycorn* by Jack London (1876–1916), published in 1913, he wrote:

> Those fifty-one days of fine sailing and intense sobriety had put me in splendid fettle.

The origin of the word 'fettle' is somewhat obscure. It probably comes from the Old English *fetel* for a belt, so 'fettle' first meant to gird oneself up, as for a heavy task.

The word was most typically used as a verb meaning to put things in order, tidy up, arrange, or prepare. Such as in Anne Brontë's (1820–49) *Agnes Grey* (1847), in the Yorkshire dialect speech of a servant:

> But next day, afore I'd gotten fettled up – for indeed, Miss, I'd no heart to sweeping an' fettling, an' washing pots; so I sat me down i' th' muck – who should come in but Maister Weston.

In northern English dialects, 'fettle' is sometimes used in the sense of making or repairing something. In Australia, a 'fettler' is a railway maintenance worker.

It is also used in some manufacturing trades – in metal casting and pottery it describes the process of knocking the rough edges off a piece.

FLAVOUR OF THE MONTH

A generic American advertising phrase of the mid 1940s attempting to persuade shoppers to buy a new flavour of ice cream each month and not just stick to their usual choice.

Since then, it has been used to describe any short-lived fashion, craze or person that is quickly dropped after a period of being in demand.

FOR THE HIGH JUMP

English slang for being in big trouble, also known these days as 'deep doo-doo' or 'deep shit'. It usually implies that dismissal or serious punishment are on the cards.

The allusion is to the hanging of a convicted criminal – the gallows being 'the high jump' – which was the former British judicial method for capital punishment.

FOR PETE'S SAKE

An exclamation of annoyance or impatience. Just who Pete is exactly remains a mystery.

The expression is perhaps an oath in the name of St Peter, the guardian of the Gates of Heaven. Saying 'for Pete's sake' might be an entreaty to the person you're saying it to, i.e. they should consider the fact that St Peter might judge them for their actions; alternatively, it may have evolved from 'for pity's sake'.

Nowadays, this particular expression of exasperation is not so frequently heard because the threshold of acceptability for more blasphemous expletives is far lower.

THE FULL MONTY

Everything, the lot, the complete works. Said of anything done to the utmost or fullest degree.

The origin of the expression is uncertain. It may derive from the 'full amount'; or the Spanish card game *monte* (literally mountain or heap of cards); or it may refer to the full, three-piece, 'Sunday best' suit from the men's outfitters Montague Burton.

The full English breakfast – bacon, eggs, sausage, black pudding, beans, fried bread … that is, the works – was popularly known as the 'Full Monty' after the Second World War. It is sometimes said this was because Field Marshal Sir Bernard Montgomery, nicknamed 'Monty' (1887–1976), was said to have started every day with a full English breakfast when campaigning in North Africa.

The British phrase became even more popular in the English-speaking world after the release of the hit 1997 film *The Full Monty,* directed by Peter Cattaneo (1964–). The movie followed a fictitious group of unemployed factory workers from Sheffield, who raise money by staging a strip act at a local club and taking off 'the full monty'.

AT FULL TILT

At full speed or with full force.

The expression probably originated in the fourteenth century, when 'tilting at the quintain' was a popular sport among medieval knights. A dummy head, often representing a Turk or Saracen, was fastened to rotate around an upright stake fixed in the ground. At full speed, the knight on horseback tilted towards the head with his lance. If he failed to strike it in the right place, it would spin round and strike him in the back before he could get clear.

Tilting at the quintain remained a rustic sport, especially popular at wedding celebrations, until the mid seventeenth century.

The similar phrase 'to tilt at windmills' has a rather different meaning, namely 'to battle fanciful enemies'. The reference is to the crazed knight Don Quixote (in Miguel de Cervantes's [1547–1616] novel, Don Quixote, *1605), who imagined the windmills to be giants and advanced to attack.*

TO GIVE SHORT SHRIFT

To treat someone peremptorily and unsympathetically, without heeding any mitigating arguments, or simply to make short work of something.

Shrift is defined as a confession to a priest. 'Short shrift' originally referred to the limited amount of time given to a convict between condemnation, confession and absolution, and then finally execution.

TO BE GIVEN THE THIRD DEGREE

This is to be the object of detailed questioning to get to the bottom of an inquiry, whether it be criminal or general.

One possible source of the phrase is Free Masonry, where the third degree is the highest level of membership. Those wishing to be considered as Master Masons must sit an intensive exam with interrogatory-style questions.

In America, the term is applied to the use by the police of exhaustive questioning to extract a confession or incriminating information from a suspect, criminal, accomplice or witness.

'Third-degree treatment' is also used as a euphemism for torture.

TO GO OFF AT HALF-COCK

To be unsuccessful at doing something due to inadequate preparation, or being in too much of a hurry – reminiscent of the phrase 'more haste less speed', or even simply 'be prepared'.

The term is related to hunting and shooting and originates from the eighteenth century, when a musket which was cocked halfway had the hammer set in the safety position to prevent accidental discharge. However, the mechanisms were sometimes faulty and the gun would fire, much to the surprise of the musketeer.

Modern sporting guns cannot in fact 'go off' at half-cock accidentally, as they no longer have a half-cock mechanism.

GORDON BENNETT

A mild oath, similar to 'Oh God'.

In fact, 'Gawd' and St Bennett (or Benet) have been put forward as the pair behind this expletive; St Benet is short for St Benedict. (Shakespeare has in *Twelfth Night* [1600], 5:1, 'the bells of St Bennet', possibly from the church, St Bennet Hithe, Paul's Wharf, opposite the Globe Theatre.)

However, it seems more likely that the said Gordon Bennett was in fact James Gordon Bennett (1841–1918), the editor-in-chief of the *New York Herald*, who, among other things, was responsible for sending Henry Morton Stanley (1841–1904) to find Dr David Livingstone (1813–73) in Africa.

Extravagant and extrovert, he gave his name to a motor race held in France in the 1900s, where he resided after a scandal in America. Such was his profile in society that there is a street in Paris named Avenue Gordon-Bennett.

In English, the similarity between Gordon and Gawd must have struck a chord. At the turn of the nineteenth century, people shied away from blasphemy in the name of God and so this curse, which is still used today, was born.

Similarly, 'Gorblimey' (later 'Cor blimey') evolved instead of 'God blind me'.

THE GREEN-EYED MONSTER

To be jealous of or to covet someone's beauty, achievements, attainments or wealth. The metaphor is commonly reduced to the expression 'to be green with envy'. The monster was identified by Shakespeare in *Othello* (1604–5; 3:3):

O! beware, my lord, of jealousy;
It is the green ey'd monster which doth mock
The meat it feeds on.

However, to accuse someone of having 'green in their eye' is to suggest that they are inexperienced or easily bamboozled, as in 'greenhorn', which means to be a novice, green behind the ears; like the green horns of a young horned animal.

Shakespeare again, in *Antony and Cleopatra* (1606–7; 1:5):

My salad days,
When I was green in judgement . . .

THE HAIR OF THE DOG

This phrase refers to a remedy usually administered to someone with a hangover, after an overindulgence of alcohol the night before. The theory is that the very thing that causes the malady is the best cure or means of relief, so another drink in the morning is considered by some the best pick-me-up (by others a recipe to make one feel worse, not better).

The general principle that 'like cures like' comes from Roman times, expressed in Latin as *similia similibus curantura*. The peculiar 'hair of the dog' phrase perhaps originated in the sixteenth century. Back then, if one was bitten by a mad dog (which was likely to be suffering from rabies), it was accepted medical practice to dress the wound with the burnt hair of the dog, as an antidote.

Amazingly, this cure was recommended for dog bites for about two hundred years before its efficacy was finally brought into question.

AS HAPPY AS LARRY

This means to be extremely happy, but the question is: 'Who was Larry?'

It is believed to be an Australian expression from the late nineteenth century, and Larry may well have been the boxer Larry Foley (1847–1917), who never lost a fight.

The word may also relate to 'larrikin', an Australian term for a young hoodlum given to acts of rowdiness. Larrikins were particularly active on the streets in the 1880s and wore distinctive colourful clothing.

AS HAPPY AS A SANDBOY

This means to be very happy or in high spirits.

It is a traditional expression from the late nineteenth and early twentieth centuries, when sandboys or sandmen drove their donkeys through the streets selling bags of sand taken from beaches. The sand was used by householders for their gardens, by builders, and by publicans for sanding their floors.

The merriness of the sandboys was probably due, in some part, to the temptation of spending their takings in the hostelries to which they delivered the sand.

HATCHES, MATCHES AND DISPATCHES

A long-established and charmingly poetic colloquialism for a newspaper's announcements of births, marriages and deaths.

TO HAVE ANTS IN ONE'S PANTS

Said of an excessively restless or over-eager person; someone displaying such behaviour can also be described as a 'fidget-bottom'.

The expression was popularized by Hugh S. Johnson (1882–1942), a dynamic former US Army general who was in charge of the National Recovery Administration (NRA) in 1933–4, when the national reconstruction policies of President Franklin D. Roosevelt's (1882–1945) 'New Deal' were implemented.

He said of the NRA general counsel Donald Richberg (1881–1960): 'Donald's agitation is just a symptom of the ants of conscience in his pants.' (N.B. 'Pants' in this case has the American meaning of 'trousers'.)

> *In Britain nowadays, the word 'pants' is often used colloquially to mean 'naff' or 'not very good', possibly harking back to the grubby English sense of the word 'pants'.*

TO HAVE A BEE IN ONE'S BONNET

To be obsessed with a particular idea or notion, as though mentally all abuzz.

The expression, in the form of the variant 'to have bees in the head', implying scattiness, was in circulation in the sixteenth century, for a reference to bees and crazed thought was recorded by the English poet, Court musician and entertainer John Heywood (*c.*1497–*c.*1580) in 1546 in one of his collections of English proverbs.

It is thought that bees first met bonnets in the poem 'Mad Maid's Song' by Robert Herrick (1591–1674), written in 1648:

> For pity, sir, find out that bee,
> Which bore my love away.
> I'll seek him in your bonnet brave,
> I'll seek him in your eyes.

TO HAVE A BONE TO PICK

This is a desire to discuss a difference of opinion, settle a misunderstanding about something disagreeable, or express a complaint. The bone is probably the bone of contention, metaphorically tossed between two dogs fighting over it.

Usage goes back to the middle of the sixteenth century, but the expression may well have come from an earlier phrase, 'to have a crow to pluck', which was used at least a hundred years earlier; the crow in this instance symbolizing discord.

In Howell's (1594–1666) *Proverbs* (1659) the phrase 'to have a goose to pluck with you' is used in the same sense.

TO HAVE A CHIP ON ONE'S SHOULDER

To display an inferiority complex, to perceive oneself as an underdog, to have a grievance, often unjustifiably.

The expression is believed to have originated in America in about 1840 and may allude to a game of dare, in which a man challenges another to dislodge a chip – as in piece of wood, not French fry – he carries on his shoulder.

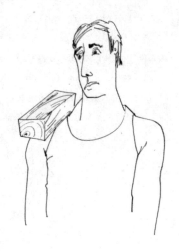

In American parlance, a chip was also a figurative term for consequences, and so the phrase may be a warning to an adversary not to aim too high.

There is an ancient proverb, 'Hew not too high lest chips fall in thine eye.' By the late sixteenth century, this health-and-safety warning had become something of a challenge, a dare to a fearless woodcutter to look high up without regard to any falling chips of wood.

TO HAVE A FIELD DAY

A figurative expression for a day or occasion or time of particular excitement, often a day away from the usual routine.

The phrase is in fact a military term for a day when troops have manoeuvres, exercises or reviews – out in the field. (The military refer to the area or sphere of operations as 'the field'.)

The term is now used more generally to mean a time of enjoyment, or making the most of things; we might say that the tabloid newspapers would 'have a field day' if they got hold of a particularly salacious story.

HERE'S MUD IN YOUR EYE!

A drinking toast, the sentiments of which could be read either way. One interpretation is that it is to wish good fortune, as it was used in the trenches of the First World War when soldiers would naturally rather mud was thrown in their eye than anything more lethal.

Another, somewhat less good-natured, theory comes from horse racing, in which, with one's own horse out in front, it will be kicking mud into the eyes of the slower runners behind.

The phrase itself is thought to originate from a Bible story – featured in chapter nine of the Gospel of St John – when Jesus puts mud in the eyes of a blind man and restores his sight.

HOIST WITH ONE'S OWN PETARD

To be beaten with one's own weapons, or to be caught in one's own trap. The modern equivalent relates to the sport of football, 'to score an own goal'.

Shakespeare coined the phrase when he wrote these lines for Hamlet:

> For 'tis the sport to have the engineer
> Hoist with his own petard.

Hamlet (1600; 3:4)

In 1600, a petard was a newly invented explosive device used for blowing up walls, barricades or gates with gunpowder. It was a metal bell-shaped grenade filled with five or six pounds of gunpowder, dug into a trench and set off by a fuse.

The devices were often unreliable and went off unexpectedly, and the engineer who fired the petard might be blown up by the explosion. Hence the expression, in which 'hoist' means to be lifted up, is an understated description of being blown up by your own bomb.

The name of the device came from the Latin petare, *meaning to break wind; the phrase is perhaps an ironic comment on the noise of the explosion.*

HOW'S YOUR FATHER?

A purely rhetorical question that originated as a humorous catchphrase in the music halls before the First World War.

It later came to be a synonym for 'nonsense' or meaningless ritual, and it is a useful substitute for a collective noun when no other comes immediately to mind (it sounds a little more imaginative than just the word 'stuff').

More recently, the phrase has acquired a sexual connotation, as in, with barely concealed innuendo, 'a bit of how's your father'.

After Bernadette Devlin's (1947–) maiden speech in the House of Commons in 1969, she commented on the ritual: 'All this stand up, sit down, kneel down and how's-your-father was so funny.'

HUE AND CRY

A noisy commotion over some spot of bother.

The phrase must have been in use since the beginning of the last millennium because the Norman French word *huer* means 'to shout'.

Until the beginning of the nineteenth century, 'hue and cry' was the old legal term for an official outcry made when calling out for assistance, 'with horn and with voice', in the pursuit of a suspected criminal escaping arrest. All able-bodied men were legally required to join the pursuit – if they refused, they risked being held liable for any theft committed by the fleeing felon. Thieves failing to respond to the 'hue and cry' were liable to greater penalties once they were caught.

We now chiefly use the phrase to describe the way the news media clamour for someone to be held responsible for high-profile crimes or political mistakes.

HUNG, DRAWN AND QUARTERED

The correct order for this form of torturous capital punishment was that the victim was 'drawn, hanged, drawn, beheaded and quartered'. The crime that merited this sort of penalty was high treason against Crown and country.

The guilty were to be 'drawn' to the place of execution on a hurdle or dragged along by horse's tail. Yet 'drawn' also meant to be disembowelled, and this was added to the punishment in between the hanging stage and the beheading stage.

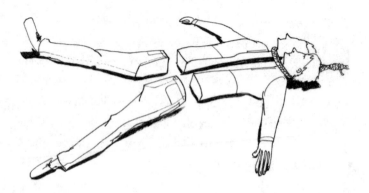

This was the sentence passed on the Scottish patriot Sir William Wallace (c.1272–1305) in August 1305: that he should be drawn from the Palace of Westminster to the Tower of London, then hanged until nearly dead, then disembowelled, then beheaded and finally quartered.

His quarters were gibbeted at Newcastle, Berwick, Stirling and Perth.

THE IRON LADY

Even before she became Prime Minister, the then Leader of the Opposition, Margaret Thatcher, was dubbed the Iron Lady.

The sobriquet was penned by the Soviet Defence Ministry newspaper *Red Star* in January 1976, in an article accusing her of trying to rekindle the Cold War through what they interpreted as a viciously anti-Soviet speech. She had said, 'The Russians are bent on world dominance . . . the Russians put guns before butter.'

The article mistakenly suggested that she was already known by this nickname in Britain, although Marje Proops *had* dubbed her 'The Iron Maiden' in the *Daily Mirror* in 1975. An iron maiden was a medieval instrument of torture in the form of a human-figure-shaped box with spiked doors that could be closed mechanically, slowly piercing its victim. (It's also the name of a popular heavy-metal group.)

Thatcher's inflammatory phrasing in her speech was, in fact, borrowed from a surprising source – one of the leaders of the Nazi Party. Hermann Goering (1893–1946) made a radio broadcast in 1936 in which he said, 'Guns will make us powerful; butter will only make us fat,' often misquoted as 'guns before butter'.

IT TAKES TWO TO TANGO

A frequently used axiom that comes from the 1952 song of this title by Al Hoffman (1902–60) and Dick Manning (1912–91):

> There are lots of things you can do alone!
> But it takes two to tango.

This satisfyingly alliterative phrase is often used in a sexual context when one partner is accused of seducing the other; it implies willingness on both sides. In general, it indicates that in any troublesome situation in which two people are involved, the blame should usually be shared between them.

It is also now used more widely in the fields of business and politics to imply that, in order to achieve agreement between two groups, both may have to compromise.

IT'S AN ILL WIND

Similar in spirit to 'every cloud has a silver lining', this ancient nautical proverb suggests that some good can come from most misfortunes. The full phrase is, 'It's an ill wind that blows nobody any good,' meaning that only the very worst situations are universally bad, and that hardships usually bring benefits eventually.

It was already widely used by 1546, when John Heywood (c.1497–c.1580) included it in his book of English proverbs. In 1591, Shakespeare wrote in *Henry VI*: 'Ill blows the wind that profits nobody' (2:5).

TO JUMP OUT OF THE FRYING PAN INTO THE FIRE

To leap from one bad predicament to another which is as bad or even worse.

In English, the phrase can be traced back to about 1530 when, in the course of a religious argument, Sir Thomas More, Henry VIII's Lord Chancellor and author of *Utopia*, said that William Tyndale (1494–1536), translator of the Bible into English, had 'featly conuayed himself out of the frying panne fayre into the fyre'.

Unfortunately, both men met a gruesome end. Sir Thomas More was hanged as a traitor in 1535 for refusing to approve the marriage between Henry VIII and Anne Boleyn, while Tyndale was publicly strangled and burned as a heretic in 1536.

> *Most languages have an equivalent phrase; the French have tomber de la poêle dans le feu – 'fall from the frying pan into the fire' – from which the English is probably translated. The ancient Greeks had, 'out of the smoke into the flame'; the Italians and Portuguese, 'to fall from the frying pan into the coals'; and the Gaelic is, 'out of the cauldron into the fire'.*

TO KEEP ONE'S POWDER DRY

To be prepared for action, but preserve one's resources until they are really needed. The phrase comes from a saying attributed to Oliver Cromwell (1599–1658), and the powder is, of course, gunpowder, which will not ignite if wet, or even damp.

During his savage Irish campaign of 1649, Cromwell is said to have concluded a speech to his troops, who were about to cross the River Slaney before attacking Wexford, with the rousing words, 'Put your trust in God, my boys, and keep your powder dry.'

There is no contemporary recording of his use of this phrase, however, and it is possible that it was coined later by the soldier and historian Valentine Blacker (1738–1823) in his poem 'Oliver's Advice', which attributed the line to Cromwell.

KEEPING UP WITH THE JONESES

This phrase defines twentieth-century materialism as the never-ending struggle to keep up with the apparent affluence of one's neighbours, paying particular attention to the cars they drive, the holidays they take, the schools their children attend and all sorts of other lifestyle indicators.

American Arthur R. Momand ('Pop'; 1886–1987), whose strip cartoon was first published in the *New York Globe* in 1913, probably invented the phrase, which he used as his cartoon's title. The strip was based on Momand's own experiences of living beyond his means in a prosperous neighbourhood – and his realization that all his neighbours were doing the same as him.

The phrase had spread to Britain by the 1940s, where its sentiments remain rampant.

TO KISS THE BLARNEY STONE

A popular term used of someone who speaks in persuasive or seductive terms; the verb 'to blarney', meaning to employ persuasive flattery, and the noun 'blarney', for 'flattering talk', have the same derivation.

The provenance for this expression can be found, literally, at Blarney Castle, near Cork, in south-west Ireland. Set high in the south wall of the castle is an almost inaccessible triangular stone bearing the inscription, *Cormac McCarthy fortis me fieri fecit*.

The tradition of kissing this Blarney Stone to improve one's eloquence and persuasive abilities – which can only be done by hanging, with one's feet securely held, head-down from the castle's battlements – dates from the eighteenth century.

The story behind the Blarney Stone's legacy is that in 1602, McCarthy, Lord of Blarney, was defending the castle against the English, who were fighting to force him to surrender the fortress and transfer his allegiance to the English crown.

However, McCarthy smooth-talked the British emissary, Sir George Carew (1565–1612), with flattery and sweet promises and stood his ground, much to the fury of Queen Elizabeth I (1533–1603).

It is said that the Queen herself coined the term 'blarney' to describe the worthlessness of McCarthy's promises.

KISS OF DEATH

This phrase derives from Judas Iscariot's kiss given to Christ in the Garden of Gethsemane before he betrayed him (Luke 23:48 and Matthew 26:49). It's also known as a 'Judas kiss', meaning an insincere act of courtesy or false affection.

In Mafia circles, a kiss from the boss may indeed be a fatal omen.

The phrase is often used today in political or business contexts, meaning that certain associations or actions may prove to be the undoing of a person or organization, or the downfall of a plan or project.

KITCHEN-SINK DRAMA

A type of drama popular in the 1950s, in which the plot centres on the more sordid aspects of working-class or lower-middle-class domestic life. Much of the action takes place in the kitchen or at the kitchen sink, which presumably is a metaphor to suggest drudgery and the dullness of dirty dishwater.

Plays such as *Look Back in Anger* (1956; this play gave rise to the phrase, 'angry young men') by John Osborne (1929–94) used such squalid settings to emphasize their message of protest against the established values of the time.

*More recently, Joanna Trollope's (1943–) stories of domestic dramas and upheavals feature the lives of the middle-class country set. Her books are known as 'Aga sagas', because much of the action takes place near the comfort of this famous stove, seen in most country kitchens **worth their salt**.*

THE LAND OF NOD

In the Bible, this was the land to which Cain was exiled after he had slain Abel (Genesis 4:16), but in modern usage, the phrase refers to the unknown place we go to in our dreams.

Jonathan Swift (1667–1745), the famous satirist, was the first to use the phrase in its figurative context in his little-known work, *Complete Collection of Genteel and Ingenious Conversation* (1731–8) – usually referred to as *Polite Conversation* – in which he wrote that he was 'going to the land of Nod', meaning that he was going to sleep.

'To nod off' also means 'to fall asleep', though this term is largely derived from the fact that the head tends to nod forward when one feels drowsy.

TO LIE ON A BED OF NAILS

A situation or position, usually self-inflicted, that is fraught with a multitude of difficult problems.

The phrase refers to the spiked bed of the Hindu *sadhu* (ascetic or holy man), on which he chooses to sleep as a mark of spiritual devotion. But while the spikes may not hurt the *sadhu*, they would be unbearable for most normal mortals.

The saying is sometimes used in its variant form, 'to lie on a bed of thorns'; both are used to describe painful situations that people have created for themselves.

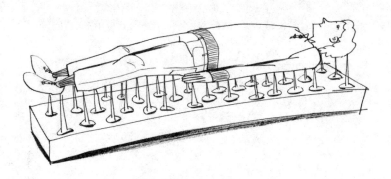

LITTLE RABBITS HAVE BIG EARS

A twentieth-century Australian modification of the old proverb 'little pitchers have great ears'. The 'ear' of a pitcher is the handle, which is often ear-shaped. The phrase 'asses as well as pitchers have big ears' is also common.

They all mean that grown-ups should watch their language when talking in front of small children, who often pick up many a hint that the speaker might wish to have passed unnoticed.

TO LIVE LIFE IN THE FAST LANE

This is a metaphor meaning to live dangerously, indulgently and expensively, and dates from the late 1970s, probably coined by newspaper headline writers.

The fast lane is the outer lane of a motorway, where traffic overtakes or travels at high speed. It is naturally associated with fast cars, and in an advertisement for Toshiba computers in 1989 the strapline read, 'Jackie Stewart lives life in the fast lane – like any businessman really.' (Stewart was three times the Formula 1 World Champion.)

The opposite metaphor, of course, is to be stranded on the hard shoulder of life.

LOVELY JUBBLY

'Jubbly' is one among many euphemisms for money. Jubbly was originally the trade name for an orange drink in the 1950s and 1960s, probably because it rhymes with bubbly. It used the slogan 'Lovely Jubbly'.

The expression came to national prominence with the popularity of the BBC comedy series *Only Fools and Horses,* which first aired in 1981, when scriptwriters who must have grown up with the slogan made it a catchphrase of Del Boy, the lovable wide boy played by David Jason (1940–).

The phrase has been repopularized in recent years by Jamie Oliver (1975–), a TV chef with a penchant for cheeky-chappie cockney slogans.

AS MAD AS A HATTER

A renowned simile ever since Lewis Carroll's (1832–98) *Alice in Wonderland* (1865), although it can be found in W. M. Thackeray's (1811–63) *Pendennis* (1850) and is recorded in America as early as 1836.

The likely reason for linking hat-makers with madness is that hatters used the chemical mercurous nitrate in the making of felt hats, and its side effects can produce trembling symptoms such as those suffered in St Vitus's Dance.

It is believed that Lewis Carroll based his character on Theophilus Carter, a furniture dealer who was known locally as the 'mad hatter' because he wore a top hat and devised fanciful inventions such as an alarm-clock bed which tipped the sleeper to the floor when it was time to wake up.

It has also been suggested that the original mad hatter was Robert Crab, a seventeenth-century English eccentric who gave all his belongings to the poor and ate only dock leaves and grass.

AS MAD AS A MARCH HARE

Lewis Carroll also refers to the madness of the March hare in *Alice in Wonderland*:

> The March hare will be much the most interesting and perhaps, as this is May, it won't be raving mad – at least not so mad as it was in March.

The phrase comes from the observation that hares run wild in March, the beginning of their rutting season, exhibiting excitable behaviour such as racing and 'boxing'.

The phrase first appeared in print in the late fourteenth century in Chaucer's *Canterbury Tales*, and has remained popular ever since, though in recent years it has been superseded by similar phrases such as 'mad as a box of frogs', or 'mad as a bag of hammers'.

MAKE DO AND MEND

An official morale-boosting slogan which has a special resonance for people of a certain age. The phrase was designed to encourage thrift and the repairing of old garments and furniture, rather than buying a brand-new replacement and using up scarce resources.

It was in common use by 1943 and set the tone for British life during the Second World War, and for many years after while food and clothing continued to be rationed.

It may have derived from 'make and mend', which was a Royal Navy term for an afternoon free from work, when the time was spent mending clothes, splicing ropes and making other minor repairs.

The slogan struck a chord in the British psyche, and although it may seem somewhat quaint to young members of today's consumer society, the economic downturn has led to something of a revival in old-fashioned frugality.

MAKE HAY WHILE THE SUN SHINES

To act promptly when the opportunity presents itself and make use of favourable circumstances (see **strike while the iron's hot**, page 169). It has a similar seize-the-day meaning to the phrases 'one today is worth two tomorrows', and, as seen on a postcard, 'there's many a lemon dries up unsqueezed.'

The phrase originated when many people worked on the land, and appeared in the sixteenth century. Before the days of the baler, cut hay was tossed about with a pitchfork before being gathered in, and then had to be left to dry in the fields, which meant that rain would spoil it.

In more recent times, it has come to be used as a justification for having fun or relaxing whenever the opportunity presents itself.

TO MAKE NO BONES

To be honest and direct without any risk that the statement may be misunderstood, but also sometimes used to mean to have no scruples about something.

One oft-cited source for this phrase is the world of gambling. Dice were often known as 'bones' because they were originally made from animal bone. Yet there is no further evidence to link the phrase to dice.

It is more likely that it has its roots in the older expression 'to find bones in something', which was used from the fifteenth century. That phrase came from the fact that finding bones in a bowl of broth was considered troublesome, so to find bones in something came to mean to take issue with it.

THE MAN ON THE CLAPHAM OMNIBUS

The man in the street. This typically ordinary person on the bus was invented by a law lord, Lord Charles Bowen (1835–94). While summing up a case for negligence, he is said to have told the jury, 'We must ask ourselves what the man on the Clapham omnibus would think.'

The phrase was first officially recorded in the law courts in 1903, when it was quoted by Sir Richard Henn Collins MR (1842–1911) in a libel case.

In Bowen's time, the omnibus was still a horse-drawn carriage and Clapham was a nondescript suburb judged to represent ordinary London.

Lord Bowen may have been inspired in his thinking by the nineteenth-century economist, essayist and journalist Walter Bagehot (1826–77), who described public opinion as 'The opinion of the bald-headed man at the back of the omnibus'.

LIKE THE *MARIE CÉLESTE*

Used to describe an eerily quiet and deserted place, somewhere normally occupied, but uncannily empty and quiet.

The *Mary Céleste* was an American brigantine found abandoned, ready to sail, between the Azores and Portugal on 5 December 1872. The ship's one lifeboat, sextant, chronometer, register and crew were missing – and no trace of any of them was ever found. It remains one of the unsolved mysteries of the high seas to this day. Hence the use of the ship's name to describe a silent, empty place.

Why 'Mary' should have become 'Marie' is open to conjecture, but it might be because of its association with the French 'Céleste'.

MORE RABBIT THAN SAINSBURY'S

Said of someone who is thought to waffle on, or to talk pointlessly. 'To rabbit' means to talk and is thought to come from cockney rhyming slang 'rabbit and pork'.

The singers Chas and Dave gave us the line 'You got more rabbit than Sainsbury's' in their song 'Rabbit', which was used in a series of TV commercials for Courage Best Bitter in Britain in the early 1980s. The advertisement poked fun at talkative women who interrupt the pleasures of supping pints of beer.

However, according to the *Oxford English Dictionary*, the term 'to rabbit' may come from a French dialect word, *rabotte*, meaning 'to waffle'.

TO MOVE THE GOALPOSTS

A colloquial expression derived from football meaning to change the agreed conditions or rules for carrying out a plan, quite often in business when clients change their minds after work on a project has already begun.

Seen in *The Guardian*, 1 March 1989, about the imposition of a new railway line in Kent:

> The people of Kent vote solidly for the Conservative Party
> ... Why are these people, therefore, trying to move the
> goalposts after the football match has started?

MY GIDDY AUNT

An exclamation of surprise, a mild oath.

It has been suggested that the expression derives from the archetypal saga of giddy-auntdom, the classic farce *Charley's Aunt* by Brandon Thomas (1856–1914), first performed in 1892: 'I'm Charley's aunt from Brazil – where the nuts come from.' 'Oh my sainted aunt' is another variant.

However, there seems to have been a fashion at the end of the nineteenth century for using the word 'giddy' in a hyperbolical sense and this too is significant. In Rudyard

Kipling's (1865–1936) *Stalky & Co* (1899) we find: 'King'll have to prove his charges up to the giddy hilt.'

This specific use of 'giddy' in the phrase suggests something or someone lightheartedly or exuberantly silly; a sense of the word that dates from the sixteenth century, as in the expression **to act the giddy goat** (see page 8). Although 'giddy' has been used for hundreds of years in this sense, at first it literally meant to be possessed by a god, but later shifted to its modern sense of experiencing vertigo or dizziness.

MY OLD DUTCH

A colloquial term for a wife or, nowadays, long-term female partner. The word is a contraction of 'duchess' and the phrase has been around since at least 1882, when it appeared in a ballad entitled 'Jimmy Johnson's Holiday' by J. F. Mitchell.

Some sources suggest that it is cockney rhyming slang, from 'Duchess of Fife', but since the first Duchess of Fife wasn't created until 1889, this explanation seems unlikely.

The expression *was* used primarily by cockneys and costermongers from the late Victorian and early Edwardian music halls, however, and gained notable currency from the song 'My Old Dutch' (1892) performed by Albert Chevalier (1861–1923), the 'costers' laureate' known as Albert the Great, who was enormously popular in his day.

MY WORD IS MY BOND

The motto of the London Stock Exchange since 1801. At the Stock Exchange, deals are made on the 'nod' without a written pledge being given, and without documents being exchanged.

The motto's Latin form is *Dictum meum pactum*, and the phrase implies a sense of honour, an agreement that cannot be broken without disgrace.

How times have changed. These days bankers are not held in quite such high regard.

NAUGHTY BUT NICE

Between 1981 and 1984 the National Dairy Council used this alliterative and somewhat suggestive slogan in a campaign to promote fresh cream cakes and the phrase is now used for anything that is a little bit wicked but enormously pleasurable.

The novelist Salman Rushdie (1947–) claimed on the BBC's *Desert Island Discs* that he had created the phrase when he was an advertising copywriter in London, but his claim was refuted by others who had worked on the account.

The phrase was certainly not new even then, as it was the title for a 1939 film about a classical-music professor who accidentally wrote a popular song, starring Dick Powell (1904–63) and Ronald Reagan (1911–2004).

It has also been used as an oblique phrase implying sexual intercourse since about 1900.

NECESSITY IS THE MOTHER OF INVENTION

An imperative need will force one to summon extra creative forces to devise a solution, or to create something, to alleviate a problem.

The phrase is thought to have been used in some form by Plato (*c.*428–348 BC) in the fourth century BC in *The Republic*, but it first appeared with the modern wording in a 1671 comedy by William Wycherley (1641–1715).

More modern derivations of the phrase are 'A guilty conscience is the mother of invention' and 'Boredom is the mother of invention'. And in a chiastic twist by one Thorstein Veblen (1857–1929), 'Invention is the mother of necessity.'

However, Daniel Defoe (1660–1731) wrote in *Serious Reflections of Robinson Crusoe* (1720):

Necessity makes an honest man a knave.

THE NINETEENTH HOLE

The bar at the golf clubhouse. The standard course has eighteen holes, so the golfer who has played badly can drown his sorrows at the nineteenth. The term was first heard by American golfers in the 1920s.

NO NEWS IS GOOD NEWS

The absence of information justifies continued optimism; that is, if all's quiet, then there is no cause for alarm. The phrase probably dates back to the early seventeenth century; in 1616, King James VI and I (1566–1625) wrote: 'No newis is bettir than evill newis.'

The word 'news', now understood as a singular noun, was still plural up to the nineteenth century, as seen in this letter from Queen Victoria to the King of the Belgians, 20 August 1861: 'The news from Austria are very sad, and make one very anxious.'

The word is in fact short for 'new stories', and the old spelling was 'newes', a literal translation from the French *nouvelles*.

NO ROOM TO SWING A CAT

A commonly used description for a restricted or cramped space.

There are various suggested origins for this phrase; 'cat' was an abbreviation for 'cat-o'-nine-tails', a whip of nine knotted lashes or 'tails', which from the eighteenth century was used in the army and navy, as well as on criminals in gaol, and was not formally banned in England as an instrument of punishment until 1948. Since space was restricted on sailing ships, whippings were carried out on deck, as there was 'no room to swing a cat' elsewhere on board.

However, while this may seem the most likely origin, 'cat' is also an old Scottish word for a rogue, and if the expression derives from this, the swing is that of the condemned criminal hanging from the gallows.

Equally, suspending live cats in leather sacks and then swinging the sacks as moving targets for archers was once a popular, if barbaric, amusement, and this too has been suggested as a source for the phrase.

NOT MY BAG

A slang expression for something which is definitely not one's subject or style.

It probably came from the American jazz scene, 'bag' meaning a personal style of playing; for instance, 'playing with a hip-hop band was not his bag'. However, the phrase came into general use, being applied to almost anything, in both America and Britain.

It shares a meaning with the more common phrase 'not my cup of tea', which has been used throughout the twentieth century to denote something that isn't to one's taste.

NOT ON YOUR NELLIE!

Not bloody likely, not on any account, on your life. One conjecture is that it derives from a cockney rhyming slang from around the 1930s, 'Nellie Duff' ('duff' rhymes with puff, i.e. breath, that which keeps you alive).

Another theory is that your 'nellie' is your stomach, your 'Aunt Nellie' – belly, something that in a more refined age you did not reveal to the world.

The phrase was one of comedian Frankie Howerd's (1917–92) catchphrases, which he popularized in the 1940s.

NOT WORTH A TINKER'S DAMN

This is one of many phrases meaning that something is worthless.

Tinkers were itinerant menders of kettles and pans and were a common sight on the streets in the eighteenth century. It has been suggested that the term comes from the tinker's custom of blocking up a hole in the article he was mending with a pellet of bread, thus making a 'dam', or plug, that would hold the molten solder. This pellet was discarded when the job was finished. So a tinker's dam is a useless or negligible thing.

However, the present spelling of 'damn' alludes to its meaning as a curse or oath, and the phrase is also heard as 'not worth a tinker's cuss', a cuss being slang for a curse, which tinkers uttered frequently.

> *It is still common 'to tinker about' with something, which means to fiddle, often in a clumsy fashion, in an attempt to make repairs.*

NUDGE NUDGE, WINK WINK, SAY NO MORE

A catchphrase understood by everyone during the 1970s, which came from the television comedy show *Monty Python's Flying Circus*, broadcast between 1969 and 1974.

Laden with sexual innuendo, these words provided the accompaniment to personal questions such as 'Is your wife a goer, then, eh, eh?' asked by a lewd character played by Eric Idle (1943–) in a ridiculously suggestive manner, accompanied by much elbow jerking, embarrassed twitching and prodding.

AS OLD AS METHUSELAH

This means to be very old indeed. Methuselah is the oldest man referred to in the Bible, and it is written in Genesis (5:27) that he died at the impossibly great age of 969 years.

'As old as the hills' is probably a more realistic simile as hills are indeed extremely ancient features of the landscape.

OLD-BOY NETWORK

This is the network of social connections established through the public-school system that were traditionally used to get on in life.

The old-school tie worn by former pupils of the public and grammar schools is a distinguishing mark, recognized by members of the same privileged class. That recognition would lead to favourable support and opportunities.

Today, the old-boy network is seen in a negative light as a way of preserving the social elite. Instead, the practice of 'networking', which involves making contacts within your chosen industry whom you hope might be able to help you get ahead, is becoming a more firmly established tool in ascending the career ladder.

ON A WING AND A PRAYER

To chance it, to hope for the best and have faith, with perhaps only small chance of success.

The phrase comes from a Second World War song by Harold Adamson (1906–80). He based his lyrics on the actual words spoken by the pilot of a damaged aircraft, who radioed the control tower as he prepared to come in to land. The 1943 song runs:

Tho' there's one motor gone, we can still carry on,
Comin' in on a wing and pray'r.

Even in his moment of panic, the pilot might have been inspired by words from Psalm 104 (v.3):

Who layeth the beams of his chambers in the waters: and maketh the clouds his chariot, and walketh upon the wings of the wind.

ON THE NAIL

This is a very old phrase meaning to pay immediately or on the spot. Generally, it means 'now', 'at once', 'exactly' or 'dead on'.

In medieval times, a nail was a shallow vessel mounted on a post or stand and business deals were closed by payments placed in the 'nail'. It is said that if a buyer was satisfied with the sample of grain shown on the nail, he paid on the spot.

Outside the Bristol Corn Exchange, such nails can still be seen in the form of four bronze pillars.

ONCE BITTEN, TWICE SHY

A phrase meaning that one learns from previous experience. Having been caught out once, one is wary or cautious the next time – and you should therefore learn from your mistakes.

'He that stumbles twice at the same stone deserves to have his shins broke' appears in R. Taverner's list of *Proverbs and Adages* of 1539, while the American humorist Josh Billings (1818–95) said that 'nobody but a fool gets bit twice by the same dog'.

The idea behind the phrase is often attributed to one of Aesop's fables, which includes the line (as translated by William Caxton [*c*.1422–92]): 'He that hath ben ones begyled by some other ought to kepe hym wel from the same.'

ONE MAN'S MEAT IS ANOTHER MAN'S POISON

This is a very old adage that simply means that what is palatable or beneficial to one person is distasteful or harmful to another.

In ancient times, meat and bread were generic terms for food, and in Britain the use of the word 'meat' in many proverbs simply meant 'food'.

The phrase 'different strokes for different folks' pretty well sums up the meaning. The rhythm and phrasing of this expression in particular have given rise to an endless stream of imitations. To an adulterer, perhaps, 'One man's mate is another man's passion,' or even 'One man's Jill is another man's thrill.'

The proverb's meaning in general has also inspired spin-offs. 'One man's floor is another man's ceiling' is attributed to D. Bloodworth (1967), while a contemporary version has a more political ring – 'one man's terrorist is another man's freedom fighter'.

ONE SANDWICH SHORT
OF A PICNIC

A derogatory description of someone who is not terribly bright. It is one of many such cartoon-like expressions, such as 'one prawn short of a cocktail' and other variations.

'The lights are on but no one's at home' and 'the lift doesn't go to the top floor' have very much the same meaning.

OUT FOR THE COUNT

Said of someone who is fast asleep, dead drunk or completely demoralized.

It is a boxing and wrestling term describing defeat by being counted out by the referee. If a fighter is floored and does not find his feet within ten seconds counted out loud, he has lost the bout.

To say 'count me out', on the other hand, means 'do not include me in this'.

OVER A BARREL

To be stuck in a helpless position, powerless to get yourself out of it, or to be at someone's mercy.

The phrase is possibly nautical in origin and is said to derive from the practice of draping over a barrel someone who has been rescued from the water when close to drowning, so encouraging the ejection of water from the lungs.

A more likely derivation, however, may be a form of punishment or torture in which the victim is bent over a barrel and beaten.

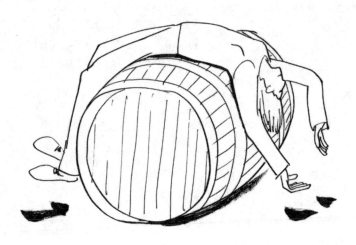

OVER THE TOP

An expression that describes something that goes way beyond the bounds of good taste or good sense, or which is outrageously inappropriate, or a complete overreaction.

It came from the trenches of the First World War, when soldiers were described as going 'over the top' when they scrambled out of the trenches to attack the enemy.

Over The Top was also the name of a television show in the 1980s, which became known only by its initials, OTT. These are still used today in many colloquial contexts in place of the original phrase.

For example, a particularly impassioned verbal outburst, or a person who behaves or dresses outrageously, might be described as 'OTT'.

TO PAINT THE TOWN RED

To go out and party, to let your hair down and enjoy an uninhibited celebration, to trip the light fantastic, perhaps even to cause some disturbance in town.

This phrase, thought to have originated in America in the 1880s, may be an allusion to a town's red-light district; that is, the area where prostitutes ply their trade, advertising with red lights in the windows of their brothels, and where rogues might begin the evening before later extending the party to the rest of town.

Alternatively, it may have been a euphemism for a rowdy night in which blood would be spilt.

PANDORA'S BOX

This is a troublesome 'can of worms' – a gift that seems of great value but is actually a curse, generating all sorts of unmanageable problems.

In Greek mythology, Pandora was the first woman, sent by Zeus as a gift to Epimetheus, who married her, against the advice of his brother Prometheus. As a wedding present, Zeus gave Pandora a beautiful box, but instructed her that she must never open it. Over time, Pandora was tempted to defy this condition ... but when she finally opened the box, all the evils of the world escaped, ever after to afflict mankind.

According to some, hope was the last thing that flew out; others believe that hope alone remained in the box.

The more modern phrase 'to open a can of worms', which was first used in America in the 1950s, is a euphemism that became popular in the UK in the 1970s.

It is a graphic metaphor for a tangled, squirming, unpleasant or uncontrollable situation that had not been apparent beforehand.

TO PASS THE ACID TEST

Said of someone or something that has been subjected to a conclusive or severe test.

The phrase was used literally during the American gold rush, when prospectors needed a sure-fire way of telling gold from valueless metals. Gold is not attacked by most acids, but reacts to nitric acid, also known as *aqua fortis*, which is therefore the acid used in the 'acid test' for gold.

To 'put on the acid' is probably derived from 'to pass the acid test' and is Australian slang meaning to exert pressure on someone when asking for a favour or a loan.

TO PASS THE BUCK

(see also **the buck stops here**, page 38)

To evade blame or responsibility and shift all criticism elsewhere. An American phrase from the game of poker, the 'buck' being the token object that is passed to the person whose turn it is to deal the next hand.

Originally, the token was a buckhorn knife, so called because its handle was made from the horn of a buck, or male deer (although some sources argue that the buck was either a piece of buckshot or a buck's tail, which early hunters carried as a talisman).

The earliest recorded use of the phrase is by Mark Twain (1835–1910) in 1872, in the first decade after the end of the American Civil War (1861–65), when poker or 'stud poker' – the stake was probably originally a stud horse – were played in bars by lumberjacks, miners and hunters, those being the days before it became known as a 'gentleman's' game.

TO PASS MUSTER

To come up to an adequate standard, to pass inspection or to get by. Originally, 'muster' was a military term for the gathering of soldiers for roll call and inspection.

To 'muster in' means to enrol, and to 'muster out' means that the group disperses or falls out.

PAST THE SELL-BY DATE

This term comes from the supermarket and is applied to perishable foods. The dates before which, for safety reasons, the goods should be sold and consumed are indicated on the packaging.

The expression is widely applied metaphorically to almost any short-lived or disposable area of life that may lose its freshness or appeal, such as ideas, fashion, relationships; it is sometimes also used of people, especially those in high-profile jobs, such as actors or models.

At the time of writing, the British Government is considering phasing out sell-by dates in an attempt to decrease the scale of the waste of perfectly good food.

A PIG IN A POKE

To buy a pig in a poke is to purchase something before you have seen it and verified its worth.

The phrase derives from an ancient form of trickery when animals were traded at market and a small suckling pig was taken for sale in a 'poke' – a word shortened from the word 'pocket', which was a stout sack.

Sales had to be agreed without opening the poke, supposedly for fear of the lively piglet escaping. Rather, people used the sealed sacks to try to palm off the runts of the litter to unsuspecting buyers, and sometimes even cats were substituted for pigs.

If the less gullible purchaser insisted on seeing the contents of the poke, the salesman might literally have to 'let the cat out of the bag' (hence that other well-known expression), and the game was up.

This form of dodgy market trading has been around for hundreds of years, and is referred to in Thomas Tusser's (1524–80) *Five Hundred Good Pointes of Husbandrie* (1580).

> *The practice was obviously widespread because other languages have similar expressions – such as the French* chat en poche *– which also refer to the folly of buying something without seeing it first. The Latin proverb* caveat emptor *– 'let the buyer beware' – warns against such underhand techniques.*

A PINCH OF SALT

To take something with 'a pinch of salt' is to treat information or explanations with great reservation, qualification, scepticism, doubt or disbelief.

A version of this phrase, 'take with a grain of salt', was in use from the seventeenth century, and is thought to stem from the popular notion that taking a small amount of salt with other ingredients was a good antidote for poison.

AS PLEASED AS PUNCH

In the traditional comic puppet show *Punch and Judy*, the pompous Mr Punch gloats smugly at the success of his evil actions and superiority over his shrewish wife Judy, and it is from this scenario that the phrase originates. Punch had a lot to be pleased about; his quick wit was triumphant even over the Devil.

The show first came to England at about the time of the Restoration in 1660. Then, it was known as *Punchinello*, which (and the name of Mr Punch himself) probably comes from the Italian *pulcinello* (young chicken).

The present Punch and Judy *scenario is similar to the original by the Italian comedian Silvio Fiorello, dating from about 1600. Although the basic plot varies, it usually involves Punch's enraged bludgeoning of his wife, Judy, their child, and several lesser characters, followed by his imprisonment … and escape, thus him being 'pleased as Punch'.*

The violence of the storylines is counteracted by slapstick action and comic dialogue.

TO POUR OIL ON TROUBLED WATERS

A well-known metaphor meaning to mollify or soothe with gentle words, or to use tact and diplomacy to restore calm after an angry or bitter argument.

It has been a well-known scientific fact since the first century AD that rough waves are calmed when oil is poured upon them. According to the Venerable Bede's (AD 673–735) *History of the English Church and People* (AD 731), St Aidan, an Irish monk of Iona, knew of this 'miracle' and gave a young priest a vessel of holy oil to pour on the sea when the waves became stormy. (The priest was on an important voyage to fetch a maiden destined to be the bride of King Oswy.)

Moreover, on his many Atlantic crossings between Pennsylvania and Portsmouth in the eighteenth century, the ever-curious Benjamin Franklin (1706–90) observed not only the Gulf Stream, but also the calming effect of oil on the waves.

PRIDE GOES BEFORE A FALL

An ancient warning for the arrogant to avoid conceit; do not be too cocksure or big-headed because events may conspire to bring you down. The phrase is shortened from the passage in Proverbs (16:18):

Pride goeth before destruction, and an haughty spirit before a fall.

> *'Pride goes before, and shame comes after'* is another form of the proverb as it was used in the sixteenth and seventeenth centuries. It has also been said that *'he who gets too big for his britches gets exposed in the end'*.

PUT A SOCK IN IT!

A plea to be quiet, to shut up, to make less noise.

It comes from the end of the nineteenth and beginning of the twentieth centuries, when the early gramophones, or 'phonographs', had large horns through which the sound was amplified. These mechanical contraptions had no volume controls, and so a convenient method of reducing the volume was to stuff a woollen sock inside the horn.

TO PUT ON THE BACK BURNER

To put off or postpone. A very useful expression in business if a decision cannot be made immediately, meaning that an idea, proposition, course of action or project can be put aside and kept in reserve for use when necessary, or when circumstances are more propitious.

It stems of course from the back burners, or rings, of a cooker, which are used for simmering, while the front burners are usually the hottest and used for fast cooking.

There is now even a verb form gaining increasing usage in office jargonese, with people talking of 'back-burnering' something.

An almost diametrically opposed metaphor is also used: an idea or project can be 'put on ice', to be figuratively defrosted at a later date.

TO PUT ONE'S FOOT IN IT

To make an inadvertent blunder, particularly to say the wrong thing and to embarrass oneself. To make a *faux pas*, which literally means 'a false step'.

The full phrase, from which this shortened version comes, is 'to put your foot in your mouth', and several sources suggest that this was first used in reference to eighteenth-century Irish parliamentarian Sir Boyle Roche (1736–1807), who in oratorical terms seems to have been the George W. Bush (1946–) of his day.

He famously delivered lines such as: 'All along the untrodden paths of the future, I can see the footprints of an unseen hand.' A contemporary is believed to have said of him, 'Every time he opens his mouth, he puts his foot in it,' and the phrase took off.

Prince Philip (1921–), who has something of a reputation for saying the wrong thing at the wrong time, calls the affliction 'dentopedalogy'.

TO BE IN QUEER STREET

Not to be confused with the gay district, this phrase means to be in financial difficulties or in dire straits.

Use of the word 'queer' could be a pun on 'query' – because Victorian tradesmen might mark the name of a customer with a poor credit rating on the ledger with a question mark.

It is more likely, however, that it is a direct translation of the German word *Querstrasse*, that is, a road at right angles to the main road.

> *Similarly, 'to be in Carey Street' is to be bankrupt. Carey Street is situated in the City of London off Chancery Lane, and is home to the bankruptcy courts.*

RAGTAG AND BOBTAIL

The riff-raff, the rabble, otherwise known as the 'great unwashed' or 'hoi polloi'; all derogatory terms for the masses or lower classes.

This expression was common in the sixteenth and seventeenth centuries as 'the rag and tag'. Rags are tatters or remnants of cloth or clothes, and a ruffian or vagabond is still known as a ragamuffin; a 'muffin' was a colloquial diminutive for a pitiful creature.

> *Rag, Tag and Bobtail were popular characters in the early days of children's television in the 1950s; they appeared on the BBC's* Watch with Mother, *and were contemporaries of* Andy Pandy *and the Flower Pot Men.*

TO READ THE RIOT ACT

Figuratively, 'to read the riot act' is to attempt to quell chattering and general commotion or misbehaviour, particularly in a group of children, by vigorous and forceful pleas coupled with threats of the consequences if order is not resumed.

The original Riot Act became law in 1715, and stated that when twelve or more people were gathered with the intention of rioting, it was the duty of the magistrates to command them to disperse, and that anyone who continued to riot for one hour afterwards was guilty of a serious criminal offence. It was not superseded until 1986 when the Public Order Act was introduced.

'To run riot' was originally said of hounds that had lost the scent, and was later applied to any group that behaved in a disorderly or unrestrained way.

THE REAL McCOY

This is a common American expression, although it originated in Scotland as 'the real Mackay', meaning 'the real thing'.

Mackay was the name of an old family descended from the Scottish people known as the Picts; the term appeared in the *Scottish National Dictionary* in 1856 as part of the phrase 'a drappie (drop) of the real Mackay'.

In the 1880s, the expression was adopted as an advertising slogan for Mackay whisky, which was exported to America and Canada, where people of Scottish origin drank it and kept the phrase alive.

In the 1890s, it was applied to a famous boxer, the prize fighter Kid 'the Real' McCoy (1872–1940), and this is the spelling that has remained in use.

Coca-Cola, probably the most advertised product in the world, adapted the phrase in the 1970s by describing their product as 'the real thing' in comparison with any rival products.

REVENGE IS A DISH BEST
SERVED COLD

Be patient, vengeance will be all the more satisfying if you take your time in getting back at someone.

There is an old proverb from 1578 that advises, 'Living well is the best revenge,' and according to Euripides (480–406 BC), 'There's nothing like the sight of an old enemy down on his luck.'

The modern wording of this phrase is often thought to come from the eighteenth-century French novel *Les Liaisons Dangereuses* by Pierre Ambroise François Choderlos de Laclos (1741–1803), as *la vengeance est un plat qui se mange froid*.

In fact, the phrase does not appear in the original novel and features only in later adaptations.

The theme of revenge has featured in art since the early Greek dramas; the most famous example in English is perhaps Shakespeare's Hamlet *(1600).*

This particular phrase was revived in 2003 as a tagline for Quentin Tarantino's revenge film Kill Bill.

TO RING THE CHANGES

This phrase comes from the world of bell ringing, which became popular in Britain in the seventeenth century and remains so to this day. It means to make variations in the way you do something.

A 'change', you see, is the order in which a series of bells is rung. Thus with a series of four bells, as in many parish churches, it is possible to ring twenty-four changes without once repeating the order in which the bells are struck $(4 \times 3 \times 2 \times 1 = 24)$.

In the nineteenth century, the phrase took on a new meaning and was used to imply that someone had been paid back for a wrongdoing or practical joke, usually by being given a taste of their own medicine.

We now most commonly use the phrase to mean simply 'to make changes' or 'to try several changes'.

The greatest number of changes ever actually rung on bells is reported to have been 40,320 changes on eight bells $(8 \times 7 \times 6 \times 5 \times 4 \times 3 \times 2 \times 1 = 40,320)$, which took about eighteen hours.

ROME WAS NOT BUILT IN A DAY

Great achievements, worthwhile tasks and the like are not accomplished without patient perseverance and a considerable passage of time.

This was originally a Latin proverb and has been quoted ever since, as in *A dialogue conteinyng the nomber in effect of all the prouerbes in the englishe tongue* (1546) by John Heywood:

Rome was not bylt on a daie (quoth he) and yet stood Tyll it was fynysht.

Rome was the greatest city in the ancient world and, according to legend, was founded in 753 BC by Romulus (hence the city's name) and his twin brother Remus. However, it is most likely to have been named from the Greek *rhoma* meaning 'strength'; its other Latin name is Valentia, from *valens* meaning 'strong'.

As an indication of its importance in the world, Rome features in numerous old sayings such as 'When in Rome, do as the Romans do' and 'All roads lead to Rome' (or 'All roads lead to rum', as W. C. Fields [1880–1946] put it).

ROUND ROBIN

A petition or protest signed in a circular form on the page so that no one name heads the list. The device is believed to have originated in seventeenth-century France and the term could be a corruption of *rond* and *ruban* – round ribbon.

The round-robin letter is believed to have been adopted by British sailors in the seventeenth or early eighteenth centuries, for use when presenting a grievance to the ship's captain. To avoid punishment, the ringleader would arrange for the signatures to be inscribed in a circular fashion around the page – although if the ship's captain was particularly vindictive, he would punish all the signatories for insurrection.

Today, we use the phrase to mean the opposite of its original meaning – it is rather a letter or email from a single author that is sent to numerous recipients.

A round-robin tournament is a friendly sporting contest, such as tennis, in which all participants change partners so that everyone competes against everyone else.

ROUND UP THE USUAL SUSPECTS

Since the film *The Usual Suspects* was released in 1994, this phrase has returned to regular use, and is employed as a jocular instruction to gather a group of people together.

It is thought that the line was first spoken in the film *Casablanca* (1943), directed by Hal B. Wallis (1899–1986) and starring Humphrey Bogart (1899–1957) and Ingrid Bergman (1889–1967). Claude Rains (1915–82), playing the French Captain Renault, Chief of Police in wartime Casablanca, delivers this classic line in a scene near the end of the movie: 'Major Strasser has been shot. Round up the usual suspects.'

When shooting began on Casablanca, *the script was not finished. Towards the end of filming, the dialogue was written on demand and literally rushed to the set.*

According to the film chronicler Leslie Halliwell (1929–91), the film 'just fell together impeccably into one of the outstanding entertainment experiences in cinema history'.

THE ROYAL 'WE'

The somewhat superior choice of the collective pronoun 'we' in place of the individual 'I' by a single person.

Legend has it that King Henry II (1133–89) was the first to employ the royal 'we' in 1169 when justifying a decision to his barons; he argued that since kings were ordained by God, his choices were God's choices too, and so used 'we' rather than 'I' when issuing his orders.

The current Queen of England, Elizabeth II, often uses this style in referring to herself, for instance during her Christmas Day broadcasts, while the frosty comment 'We are not amused' was attributed to Queen Victoria in 1900.

In March 1989, the then Prime Minister, Margaret Thatcher, announced to the world in a famously regal tone:

We have become a grandmother.

TO RUB SALT INTO THE WOUND

To increase someone's pain or shame.

The phrase alludes to an ancient nautical punishment for misbehaviour by members of a ship's crew. Errant sailors were flogged on the bare back, and afterwards salt was rubbed into the wounds. Salt is a well-known antiseptic, so it helped to heal the lacerations, but it also made them much more painful.

An extension of this phrase is the saying 'Don't rub it in,' an admission that one may have made a fool of oneself, but people should not carry on reminding one.

RULE OF THUMB

A rough guesswork measure, a calculation based on generally held experience in a certain field. This rule is distinct from any proven theory.

It refers to the use of the thumb to make rough measurements. The first joint of the average adult thumb measures 1 inch or 25 mm, so could be used to measure objects quickly that were close at hand; while raising the thumb and aligning it with distant objects was a common way of estimating how far off they were.

There is also an apochryphal derivation for 'rule of thumb': in the days when it was accepted practice for a man to beat his wife, the stick for this purpose was legally allowed to be no broader than the thickness of a man's thumb; it was illegal for the stick to be thicker and a man using such a stick could be arrested for assault.

TO RUN THE GAUNTLET

To be attacked on all sides or, in modern use, to be severely criticized or to try to extricate oneself from a situation while under attack on all sides.

The expression appeared in English at the time of the Thirty Years War (1618–48) as 'gantlope', meaning the passage between two files of soldiers. It is an amalgamation of the Swedish words *galop* (passageway), *gata* (way), and *lop* (course).

'Running the gauntlet' was a form of punishment said to have originated in Sweden amongst soldiers and sailors. The company or crew, armed with whips, thongs or rods, were assembled in two facing rows, and the miscreant had to run the course between them, while each man dealt him as severe a blow as he thought befitted the misdemeanour.

Native Americans also had a similar, more brutal, form of retribution, because here the victim was not intended to survive the blows he suffered during his run.

TO SAIL CLOSE TO THE WIND

This is another of the many proverbs that come from life on the high seas. It is a figurative term, still in use today, meaning to take a chance, to emerge from an escapade just within the letter of the rule book, or, more riskily, to push the limits of what decency or propriety allows.

The nautical expression refers to the practice of steering a ship as near as possible to the point from which the wind is blowing, while keeping the sails filled.

To 'sail against the wind' is to go against the trend, in opposition to current thinking, practice or fashion. And to 'sail before the wind' is to prosper, to meet with great success, just as a ship sails smoothly and rapidly with a following wind.

Similarly, to 'sail into the wind' is to tackle a difficult task with great vigour and directness.

THE SANDS ARE RUNNING OUT

A metaphor to remind us that time is short; there will be less time to do what you have to do unless you act now. The phrase is frequently used with reference to someone who has not much longer to live.

The allusion is to the sand in an hourglass. The original version of the phrase is 'the sands of time are running out', the first part of which appears in the poem 'A Psalm of Life' (1838) by Henry Wadsworth Longfellow (1807–82):

> Lives of great men all around us,
> We can make our lives sublime,
> And, departing, leave behind us
> Footprints on the sands of time.

Or as Robert Burns (1759–96) wrote in 'Tam o' Shanter' in 1791:

> Nae man can tether time or tide.

This is a variant of the old (c.thirteenth-century) English proverb 'Time and tide wait for no man.'

TO SAVE ONE'S BACON

To have a narrow escape, to be rescued from some dire situation without injury or loss.

This expression dates from the late seventeenth or early eighteenth century when bacon was a significant part of the diet.

According to Nathan Bailey's *Universal Etymological English Dictionary* of 1720, 'bacon' was also a slang term to describe booty of any kind which fell to beggars, petty thieves, highwaymen and the like in their enterprises. Bacon thus became synonymous with livelihood, so 'to save someone's bacon' therefore took the meaning 'to save a person'.

'To bring home the bacon', meaning to earn the money to maintain the household, describes the custom at country fairs of greasing a live pig and letting it loose among a group of blindfolded contestants. Whoever successfully caught the greased pig could keep it and so 'bring home the bacon'.

SAVED BY THE BELL

This is a boxing term thought to date from the late nineteenth century. A floored contestant being counted out (see **out for the count**, page 119) might be saved by the ringing of the bell marking the end of the round, giving him the three-minute break between rounds to recover.

However, there is another, albeit unsubstantiated, and rather gruesome theory to explain this phrase. When graveyards became overcrowded in the eighteenth century, coffins were dug up, the bones taken away and the graves reused.

In reopening the coffins, one out of twenty-five was found to have scratch marks on the inside, meaning that its occupant must have been buried alive.

To guard against this most unfortunate occurrence in the future, a string was tied to the wrist of the corpse, which led from the coffin and up through the ground, where it was tied to a bell. Someone would have to sit in the graveyard all night to listen for the bell – hence the phrase 'saved by the bell'.

From the same derivation, we have night workers on the 'graveyard shift' and sailors on the 'graveyard watch' between midnight and dawn.

TO SEE A MAN ABOUT A DOG

This is a very shifty turn of phrase and suggests a desire to cover up one's real actions. It is the excuse offered if one wishes to be discreet and avoid giving the true reason for leaving the room, the meeting or whatever social gathering.

The phrase is sometimes used as a euphemism for some unmentionable activity such as going to the lavatory – or worse, going to do something or meet someone one shouldn't.

The phrase originally referred to betting on dog racing.

TO SEE RED

To give way to excessive passion or anger, or to be violently moved; to indulge in physical violence while in a state of frenzy.

The reference is to the Spanish spectacle of bullfighting and the art of taunting the bull. The phrase 'like a red rag to a bull' is said of anything that is calculated to excite rage. Toreadors' capes are lined with red (although there is actually no evidence to suggest that the colour itself incenses the bulls).

The phrase may also have blended with an American term in use in the early 1900s, 'to see things red', which describes the feeling of anger when the blood rises, or the 'red mist' descends.

TO SEE THROUGH ROSE-TINTED SPECTACLES

To look at life or to regard circumstances with unjustified optimism, always looking on the bright side of life, as though it were suffused with a gentle pink light. Spectacles of such a hue would show the world 'in the pink' – but it would be misleadingly rosy, bright and hopeful.

The French equivalent is *voir la vie en rose* – again, to see life 'in the pink', which in turn means to be in excellent health (abbreviated from the phrase 'in the pink of health' or 'in the pink of condition', a definition derived from a flower in its best state).

TO SELL SOMEONE DOWN THE RIVER

This expression means to deceive or to betray. The phrase probably originated in the first few years of the nineteenth century in the Southern states of America.

Since by then it was illegal to import slaves, there was an internal trade and they were brought down the Mississippi to the slave markets of Natchez or New Orleans. Therefore if a slave was 'sold down the river', he lost his home and family.

The saying particularly alludes to the practice of selling unruly slaves to owners of plantations on the lower river, where conditions were harsher than in the more northerly slave states.

To 'sell' is old slang for 'swindle' or 'hoax', and a person who has been tricked is said to have been 'sold'.

To 'sell the pass' is to betray one's own side; the phrase was originally Irish and is applied to those who turn king's evidence or who betray their comrades for money.

The tradition relates to the behaviour of the regiment that was sent by Crotha, Lord of Atha, to hold a pass against the invading army of Trathal, King of Cael. The pass was yielded for money and Trathal, victorious, assumed the title of King of Ireland.

TO SELL OFF THE FAMILY SILVER

To dispose of long-held and valuable assets for immediate short-term gain. This phrase comes from a speech made by former Conservative Prime Minister Sir Harold Macmillan (1894–1986) to the Tory Reform Group in 1985.

Though in favour of privatization in principle, he objected to methods used by Margaret Thatcher's government and to the use of the profits of the sales of Britain's big industries as if they were income.

'First of all the Georgian silver goes, and then all that nice furniture that used to be in the saloon. Then the Canalettos go,' he said, likening the process to the selling off of prized heirlooms by aristocratic families desperate for a quick injection of cash.

The term is now common shorthand for the selling of state-owned resources to private companies.

TO SEND SOMEONE TO COVENTRY

To refuse to speak to someone, to ostracize a person or to ignore them.

At the time of the Great Rebellion (or English Civil War) between 1642 and 1649, Royalists were often taken to Coventry to be imprisoned. The story goes that because the city was strongly Protestant and pro-Parliament, the local people would shun the incoming Cavaliers, so when a soldier was sent to Coventry, he would be given 'the cold shoulder'.

Edward Hyde, Earl of Clarendon (1609–74), referred to Royalist prisoners captured in Birmingham who were 'sent to Coventry' – effectively into exile.

To take this a step further, to refuse to have any dealing with a person or group of people as a means of protest or coercion is to 'boycott' them, a term which dates from 1880, when such methods were used by the Irish Land League against one Captain C. C. Boycott (1832–97), a land agent in County Mayo, to try to persuade him to reduce rents.

TO SEPARATE THE SHEEP FROM THE GOATS

To divide the worthy from the unworthy, the favoured from the disfavoured, the good from the bad. The phrase comes from the Bible, where sheep represent the flock of Christ, while goats symbolize virility, lust, cunning and destructiveness, and, often, the Devil.

> And before him shall be gathered all nations; and he shall separate them one from another, as a shepherd divideth his sheep from the goats.
>
> Matthew 25:32

A similar expression, also from the Bible, is 'to separate the wheat from the chaff', meaning to distinguish good from bad. A more modern version is 'to separate the men from the boys'.

TO BE IN SEVENTH HEAVEN

To be supremely happy, in a state of complete ecstasy.

The seventh heaven was defined by the Kabbalists – students of a Jewish mystical system of theology and metaphysics with its roots in ancient Greek teachings, which dates from the eleventh and twelfth centuries, and from which Madonna's famous version of Kabbalah stems.

The Kabbalists interpreted passages from the Old Testament based on the symbolism of numbers, devised and decoded charms and created mystical anagrams and the like. They maintained that there were seven heavens each rising above the other; the seventh being the home of God and the archangels, the highest in the hierarchy of the angels.

Seven is a mystic or sacred number. It is the sum of four and three which, among the Pythagoreans, were, and have been ever since, counted as lucky numbers. Among ancient cultures, there were seven sacred planets.

The Hebrew verb 'to swear' means literally to 'come under the influence of seven things', while in an Arabic curse, seven stones are smeared with blood. All of which demonstrate the power of seven as a mystical number.

AT THE SHARP END

Directly involved with the action, positioned where the competition or danger is greatest. The connection is not with the point of a sword, but with the pointed shape of the bows of a ship, which are the first towards the enemy at the start of any engagement or battle.

The cry of 'Look sharp!' or 'Sharp's the word!' are both calls to immediate action, whether on the battlefield or in the playground; the expressions also mean to be observant, to 'keep your eye on the ball'.

Before the days of large supermarkets and closed-circuit television, if a shopkeeper suspected a customer of shoplifting, he would give a coded warning to his assistant by saying, 'Mr Sharp has come in.'

TO SHOOT THE MOON

This is an American expression meaning to leave without paying one's bills or rent, or to remove swiftly one's household goods under cover of night to avoid their seizure by a landlord or creditor. It's more colloquially known as 'to do a moonlight flit' and is often shortened to 'do a moonlight' or even 'to flit'.

Simply 'to moonlight', however, means to take a second – secret – job, supposedly at night, to supplement one's wages from the day job.

> *References to the moon are often used to denote that something is fanciful: for instance, unrealistic ideas are known as 'moonshine'; 'to cry for the moon' means to crave what is totally beyond one's reach.*

TO SHOW A LEG

The summons to 'show a leg' or 'shake a leg' is a morning wake-up call. It is a naval phrase and was the traditional alarm call used to rouse the hands from their hammocks.

It comes from the days in the mid nineteenth century when women were allowed to sleep onboard ship when the navy was in port. At the cry of 'Show a leg!', if a woman's limb was shaken out of the hammock, she was allowed to lie in, but if the hairy leg of a rating appeared, he had to get up and get on with his duties.

Later in the nineteenth century, to 'shake a leg' came to mean 'to dance', while in America it meant 'to hurry up'.

AS SICK AS A PARROT

A term to describe extreme disappointment at an unexpected failure or setback. A similar phrase, 'melancholy as a parrot', was used by the author Aphra Behn (1640–89) in the seventeenth century, and it is to describe this kind of malady, rather than sickness to the stomach, that the phrase is used today.

In the 1970s and 1980s, it was a somewhat overused metaphor favoured by football managers, who often employed it to describe their feelings after losing a match. This surge in use of the phrase may have been linked to scare stories in the press at the time about the highly contagious disease psittacosis or 'parrot fever', which could be passed from birds kept as pets to their human owners.

Despite being mocked by the satirical magazine *Private Eye*, though perhaps helped by the absurdity of the 'Dead Parrot' sketch in *Monty Python's Flying Circus*, the phrase caught the public imagination and is still common, though it has been superseded in some circles by the more economical 'gutted'.

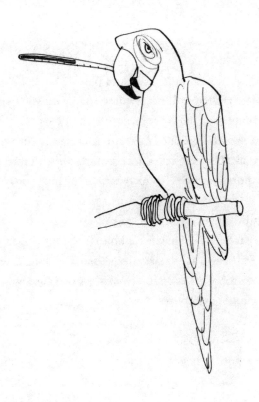

TO SIT ABOVE THE SALT

To sit in a place of distinction at the dinner table.

Formerly, the family 'saler' or salt cellar was an ornate silver centrepiece, placed in the middle of the table. Special or honoured guests of distinction sat above the saler – that is, between the salt and the head of the table where the host sat – while dependants and not-quite-so-important personages sat below.

THE SIXTY-FOUR-THOUSAND-DOLLAR QUESTION

The ultimate and most difficult question, the nub of a problem.

This widely used phrase comes from the 1940s American radio quiz show, *Take It or Leave It*. During the course of the show, contestants were asked increasingly difficult questions for prize money, which also increased as the questions became harder. The final question was worth $64.

Naturally, inflation has affected this expression over the years since it began life as the humble sixty-four-dollar question, growing first to sixty-four thousand dollars and recently to sixty-four billion. The expression is used in all English-speaking countries.

A SKELETON IN THE CLOSET

A domestic source of humiliation or shame which a family or individual conspires to conceal from others. Every family is said to have one, and certainly these days it seems that every public figure does too, whether it is in the form of an ex-mistress or lover, or some ancient but discreditable financial scam.

The expression seems to have been in use from the early 1800s and may have derived from the gothic horror stories popular at the time, in which murders were concealed by hiding the corpse in a cupboard, or bricking it up in a wall. In 1853, it appeared in the figurative sense in *The Newcomes* by William Makepeace Thackeray:

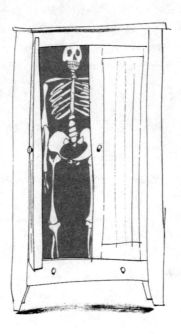

And it is from these that we shall arrive at some particulars regarding the Newcome family, which will show us that they have a skeleton or two in their closets as well as their neighbours.

An apocryphal source of the phrase is a story in which a person without a single care or trouble in the world had to be found. After a long search, a squeaky-clean lady was found, but to the great surprise of all, after she had proved herself on all counts, she went upstairs and opened a closet, which contained a human skeleton.

'I try and keep my trouble to myself, but every night my husband makes me kiss that skeleton,' she said. She then explained that the skeleton was that of her husband's rival, killed in a duel over her.

TO BE ON SKID ROW

An American expression applied to the part of town frequented by vagrants, hobos, alcoholics and down-and-outs. Hence if you are 'on the skids', it means that you are on your way to that rather grimy quarter of the city, about to skid off the path of virtue and respectability.

The expression probably comes from the early days of the Seattle timber industry. A 'skid row' was a row of logs down which other felled timber was slid or skidded. Tacoma, near Seattle, became prosperous with the growth of the timber industry, and in due course there were plentiful supplies of liquor and brothels in the town, close at hand for lumberjacks working the skid row.

SLING YOUR HOOK!

A somewhat forceful command urging a person to leave; a way, without resorting to foul language, of asking someone to go away.

The expression is probably of nautical origin and alludes to the anchor, or 'hook', which must be secured in its sling at the bow before the ship can cast off.

Other forms of the expression – 'Hook it!' and 'Take your hook!' – are also used, perhaps to give emphasis to one's wish that a person should leave and set about their business.

AS SNUG AS A BUG IN A RUG

A whimsical and comfortable comparison dating from the eighteenth century, although a 'snug' is a sixteenth-century word for a parlour in an inn.

The phrase is usually credited to Benjamin Franklin, who wrote it in 1772 as an epitaph for a pet squirrel that had belonged to Georgiana Shipley, the daughter of his friend, the Bishop of St Asaph.

Franklin's wife had sent the Shipleys the grey squirrel as a gift from Philadelphia and they named him Skugg, a common nickname for squirrels at the time. Tragically, he escaped from his cage and was killed by a dog. Franklin wrote:

Here Skugg
Lies snug
As a bug
In a rug.

However, there are earlier uses, as in a celebration of David Garrick's (1717–79) 1769 Shakespeare festival. Seen printed in the *Stratford Jubilee*:

If she [a rich widow] has the mopus's [money],
I'll have her, as snug as a bug in a rug.

And there are several similar variations from which the phrase may have sprung. In 1706, Edward Ward (1667–79) wrote in *The Wooden World Dissected*:

He sits as snug as a bee in a box.

And in Thomas Heywood's (*c.*1574–1641) 1603 play *A Woman Killed with Kindness*, there is:

Let us sleep as snug as pigs in pease-straw.

SOMEWHERE TO THE RIGHT OF GENGHIS KHAN

This cliché describes someone whose views are extremely right wing.

Genghis Khan (1162–1227) was the founder of the Moghul Empire. His original name was Temujin and he was given the title 'Genghis Khan', which literally means 'King of the Ocean'. He acquired a fighting force of some 20,000 tribesmen and through military skill, sheer brutality, and relentless raping and pillaging, overcame the Mongolian and Tartar peoples, and by 1206 he was acknowledged overlord of Mongolia.

Eventually, his empire extended from China to the Adriatic Sea and his son reached the walls of Budapest.

Arthur Scargill (1938–), president of the National Union of Mineworkers, said in 1982, 'Of course, in those days, the union leaders were well to the right of Genghis Khan.'

SOUR GRAPES

This is an ancient metaphor used when someone denigrates something that is clearly desirable because they know they can't have it for themselves.

The phrase comes from the well-known fable 'The Fox and the Grapes' by Aesop, dated to the sixth century BC:

One hot day, a thirsty fox spotted some juicy-looking grapes hanging from a vine. The cluster of fruit was just out of reach. However hard he tried, he could not reach the grapes; and the greater the effort he made, the hotter and thirstier he became.

Eventually, the fox gave up and reasoned that as the grapes were beyond reach, they would probably be sour and inedible.

The moral of the story is that we can console ourselves with the fact that, although some things are unattainable, we probably wouldn't like them anyway.

TO SOW DRAGON'S TEETH

To stir up trouble, strife or war, or to foster disagreement.

The reference is to the Greek myth of Cadmus. Cadmus was supposed to have introduced the alphabet to Greece and, according to legend, he killed the dragon that guarded the fountain of Dirce, in Bœotia, and sowed its teeth in the ground.

From these sprang up a horde of warriors intent on killing him. On the goddess Athene's advice, Cadmus threw a precious stone among them. The warriors set upon each other in the struggle to retrieve the stone until only five remained alive, and with Cadmus they founded Thebes.

The teeth which Cadmus did not sow came into the hands of Aetes, King of Colchis, and one of the tasks he gave the hero Jason – he of the *Argo* and the Golden Fleece – was to sow them and slay the armed warriors that rose from them.

TO SPILL THE BEANS

The expression means 'to let on', to tell all – perhaps prematurely – to an eager audience, to give away a secret or 'to let the cat out of the bag' (see **a pig in a poke**, page 126).

There are various explanations for the derivation, one of the most colourful being that it may have originated at the turn of the twentieth century as an American euphemism for vomiting, because beans represented basic food.

Another possibility is that the phrase comes from ancient Greek voting practices, where black and white beans were used to represent agreement and disagreement with the issue being voted on. Each voter put one bean into a pot or helmet – and the result was revealed by spilling out the beans.

Beans appear in various expressions: 'to be full of beans' means to be in high spirits or full of energy, and was originally said of lively horses; beans used to be slang for money or property, so that 'I haven't got a bean' means that one is broke.

SPIN DOCTOR

This phrase comes from baseball and refers to the spin put on the ball by a pitcher to disguise its true direction or confuse the batter.

It is an American idiom which was first applied in political commentary in the mid 1980s during Ronald Reagan's presidency, describing his public-relations advisers during promotion of the 'Star Wars' Strategic Defence Initiative (SDI).

These so-called 'spin doctors' were on 'spin control', their mission being to give the preferred interpretation of events to the world's media, thereby manipulating public opinion in the desired direction. The spin doctor is now a prominent feature of British politics and business in general.

TO STAND IN ANOTHER MAN'S SHOES

'To stand in another man's shoes' is to take the place of another person empathetically.

In similar vein, the opportunistic phrase 'waiting for dead men's shoes' is sometimes thought, if not spoken.

Among the Vikings, when a man adopted a son, the adoptee put on the shoes of his new father.

Reynard the Fox, *a medieval beast epic (c.1175–1250), is a satire on contemporary life found in French, Flemish and German literature. Reynard, having turned the tables on the former minister Sir Bruin the Bear, asks the Queen to let him have the shoes of the disgraced bear. As a result, Bruin's shoes are torn off and put on the new hero.*

TO STEAL SOMEONE ELSE'S THUNDER

To adopt someone else's own special methods or ideas as if they were one's own. The story behind the origin of this phrase was recounted by the eighteenth-century actor-manager, playwright and Poet Laureate Colley Cibber (1671–1757) in his *Lives of the Poets* (1753), and was also mentioned by Alexander Pope (1688–1744) in his poem *The Dunciad* (1728).

Legend has it that John Dennis (1657–1734), an actor-manager of the early part of the eighteenth century, had invented a machine to make stage thunder, which he employed in his own play, *Appius and Virginia*, performed at the Drury Lane Theatre in London in 1709.

However, Mr Dennis, whatever his inventive talents, was not a particularly gifted playwright; the play did not fill the house and was soon taken off in favour of a production of *Macbeth* by another company.

Dennis went to their opening night and was astonished to hear his thunder machine in action. He leapt to his feet and shouted, 'That is my thunder, by God; the villains will play my thunder but not my play!'

Since the eighteenth century, the phrase has subsequently been refined to become 'to steal one's thunder'.

STIFF UPPER LIP

A determined resolve combined with complete suppression of the emotions.

This is supposedly a traditional characteristic of the English, especially military officers during the two world wars. Their upper lips were frequently concealed with a moustache, which perhaps became fashionable because it could conceal any uncontrollable trembling reflexes at the wrong moment. A quivering upper lip is often deemed a sign of emotion.

It is not clear when the phrase was first heard, but despite its associations with English reserve, it is in fact thought to be of American origin. It certainly appeared well before the First World War in the work of American poet Phoebe Cary (1824–71) in 'Keep a Stiff Upper Lip':

And though hard be the task,
'Keep a stiff upper lip.'

STILL WATERS RUN DEEP

However quiet or calm someone may seem on the surface, do not be deceived: there is probably great depth of knowledge, personality or a hot temper lurking below.

This is a Latin proverb, thought to come from *Cato's Morals*. The version we use today was first printed in an anonymously authored Middle English verse work 'Cursor Mundi' ('Runner of the World'; *c.*1300), which includes the line: 'There the flode is deppist the water standis stillist.'

The Malayan proverb, 'Don't think there are no crocodiles because the water is calm,' means much the same.

It is never a good idea to show off or talk too much, because as everyone knows, empty vessels make the most noise. Speech is silver, but silence is golden.

STRAIGHT FROM THE HORSE'S MOUTH
(see also **don't look a gift horse in the mouth**, page 60)

Some knowledge received direct from the highest authority, from the person whose word need not be doubted.

The expression comes from horse racing, where the tips to be trusted came from those closest to the breeders and trainers. The phrase implies that you've heard something from the best possible source – in this case, the horse itself.

A variation on this as a source is the idea that the true age of a horse can be ascertained by an examination of its mouth. The first permanent horse teeth appear in the centre of the jaw at the age of two and a half. A year later, a second pair appears, and at between four and five years, the third pair appears.

So, no matter what an owner may say about a horse's age, the evidence is in the horse's mouth.

STRIKE WHILE THE IRON'S HOT

To act immediately when the opportunity arises. This is a metaphor from the blacksmith's shop, since iron cannot be easily worked once it has cooled down.

The phrase has been attributed to Geoffrey Chaucer, although there are many ancient sayings that encourage action today rather than waiting for tomorrow. Pittacus (c.640–568 BC) said, 'Know thy opportunity,' while **make hay while the sun shines** (see page 104) appears in an early sixteenth-century book of proverbs.

More up to date, a women's-lib slogan neatly inverts the proverb in a warning against inaction: 'Don't iron while the strike is hot.'

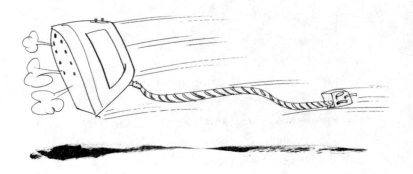

SUCK IT AND SEE

Said of anything experimental, the saying alludes to taking a pill, which has to be sucked first to see if it works.

The expression was a catchphrase of Charlie Naughton (1886–1976) of the Crazy Gang (a group of British entertainers from the 1930s), and probably originated earlier in the music halls.

> To say that something 'sucks' is a derisive description of something bad or of someone's failure.
>
> A 'sucker', meanwhile, is someone who is easily deceived, a greenhorn; that is, a newborn creature that still suckles at its mother's breast.

SWEET FANNY ADAMS

This expression is ambiguously used to mean either nothing at all, or sweet nothing. It has a very tragic origin.

In 1867, eight-year-old Fanny Adams was raped and murdered in a hop garden in Alton, Hampshire, and her dismembered body was thrown into the River Wey. A twenty-one-year-old solicitor's clerk, Frederick Baker, was tried soon after and hanged at Winchester.

The Royal Navy, with extreme black humour, adopted the poor girl's name as a synonym for tinned mutton, which was first issued at this time, and for a while stewed meat was known as Fanny Adams. 'Sweet Fanny Adams' became, as a consequence, a phrase for anything worthless, and subsequently to mean nothing at all.

The phrase is still used today, usually as just the initials 'SFA' or 'sweet FA', which happen to be the same as 'f**k all', from which most people, wrongly, think this expression is derived.

THE SWORD OF DAMOCLES

Impending danger or disaster in the midst of great prosperity or good fortune.

In the fourth century BC, Damocles, who was a toadying sycophant of Dionysus the Elder of Syracuse (see **the walls have ears**, page 183), was invited by the tyrant to test his self-proclaimed charm and wit. Damocles accepted and was treated to a sumptuous banquet, but over his head a sword was suspended by a mere hair, intended by Dionysus as a symbolic indicator of the fragility of wealth and power, his own included.

This quite naturally inhibited Damocles's performance at the banquet because he was too frightened to move.

TO TAKE A DEKKO

To glance at, or to have a quick look at.

This is one of the many phrases that were brought back from India by the British Army in the colonial days in the late nineteenth century. In Hindi, *dekho* is the imperative form of the verb *dekhna*, meaning 'to look at'.

TO TAKE AN EARLY BATH

This euphemism comes from the football pitch, and means to retire early to the dressing room after being sent off by the referee, or being injured during a match (of football or rugby).

Football has been around in the UK since at least 1170 and the original game was generally bloody and brutal, but in 1863 the Football Association was established as a governing body of the game. In 1881, it introduced a new law stating that if a player was guilty of 'ungentlemanly behaviour', the referee could order him off the ground.

By the time club football had become firmly established in the 1920s and 1930s, and clubs had their own facilities for the players, it was customary for the players to share a bath together after the match and thus the phrase arose.

By the 1950s, radio and TV commentators of both soccer and American football in the US were using the expression.

It passed into more general use to describe any situation in which someone is obliged to pull out of the action before it is over. In America, and increasingly in this country, 'to take a bath' means to suffer any kind of defeat or serious loss, as in 'he took a bath in the stock-market collapse', while the original phrase has evolved with the times into 'to take an early shower'.

TO TAKE FORTY WINKS

A colloquial term for a short nap or a doze.

Quite why shutting one eye forty times has come to mean a quick snooze is unclear, but it could have something to do with the fact that the number forty appears frequently in the scriptures and used to be thought of as a holy number.

Moses was on the Mount for forty days and forty nights; Elijah was fed by ravens for forty days; the rain of the Flood fell forty days, and another forty days passed before Noah opened the window of the ark. Christ fasted for forty days and he was seen forty days after his Resurrection.

Modern colloquialisms for a quick nap include a 'zizz' or 'to catch a few zeds' – alluding to the 'Zzz's drawn in cartoons indicating that the character is asleep. Busy people and politicians who work late into the night maintain their faculties by taking 'power naps' to recharge their batteries.

TO TAKE FRENCH LEAVE

This is leave of absence without permission or without announcing one's departure.

Rivalry between the British and the French has lasted for hundreds of years and this phrase is thought to have originated during the Napoleonic wars. It was a deliberate slight, suggesting that French soldiers had a habit of taking unauthorized leave, implying that they were lazy or disloyal.

The term is still sometimes used among British soldiers today to mean desertion. A modern variant is 'AWOL' (pronounced 'ay-woll'), from the military acronym for 'absent without leave'; if an AWOL serviceman does not return fairly swiftly, he will face the much more serious charge of desertion.

In general, however, we now use 'to take French leave' as a euphemism for leaving without saying goodbye to one's host at a party.

Not to be outdone, the French later associated this latter habit with the English: hence their equivalent for 'French leave' is s'en aller à l'anglaise.

An earlier French insult was the sixteenth-century slang for a creditor, which was un Anglais. *Even Shakespeare got in on the insult-the-French act:*

France is a dog hole.

All's Well That Ends Well *(1623; 3:2)*

TO TAKE A RAIN CHECK

A rain check is the receipt or counterfoil of a baseball ticket that can be used at a later date if a game has been interrupted by rain. It is an American expression and the phrase retains the American spelling of 'cheque'.

The phrase is now often used figuratively, to put an invitation on hold and defer it until a later date. It is, in fact, a polite way of postponing something indefinitely, with only a minor commitment to rearrange.

TO BE TAKEN FOR A RIDE

This colloquial phrase can be interpreted in one of two ways. It refers either to the victim of a light-hearted joke, prank or con, or – in its sinister and probably original meaning, a completely genuine use of the phrase – to someone who is taken for a ride somewhere and does not come back in one piece, if at all.

The rival underworld gangs of major American cities in the 1920s and 1930s were virtually at war with each other, and any unfortunate who was unlucky enough to tempt the wrath of the gang leader, or Don in the case of the Mafia, would be literally taken for a ride in a limousine, ostensibly to discuss certain matters or sort out some misunderstanding. He would be very unlikely to return alive, however – or, indeed, to return at all.

TO TALK TURKEY

To discuss some subject frankly or seriously.

The origin of the expression is uncertain, but it is thought to date back to nineteenth-century America and may have arisen from the efforts of turkey hunters to attract their prey by making gobbling noises. The birds would then either emerge from their cover or return the call, so revealing their whereabouts.

At the turn of the last century, the turkey was considered an amusing bird, and conversations in which one 'talked turkey' were convivial. A young suitor's chat-up lines would also be called 'talking turkey', perhaps because in a fit of nerves he might become tongue-tied and his words would come out like gobbling noises.

Later, the meaning became more serious and related to stern admonitions.

Incidentally, turkeys do not come from Turkey, but from North America, and were brought to Spain from Mexico. Benjamin Franklin suggested the turkey should be the emblem of the United States of America – however, the bald eagle was chosen instead.

THAT TAKES THE BISCUIT!

An exclamation to indicate shock and surprise at some action that has gone beyond the bounds of expectation.

Specially spiced biscuits and cakes were formerly prized as small treats and were given as rewards in a variety of competitions. This phrase is thought to be a derivation of 'that takes the cake', which in the Deep South of America in the 1920s referred to a winning performance at a cake walk.

This version of the phrase may predate cake walks by several thousand years, however, as there is evidence to suggest that 'taking the cake' was synonymous with taking victory as early as the fifth century, when 'cakes' were small pyramids of grains and honey.

In *The Knights*, Aristotle (384–322 BC) wrote: 'If you surpass him in impudence, then we take the cake.'

AS THICK AS THIEVES

To be intimate with some person or group, to be in collusion with them. 'Thick' is used in this context to mean 'closely knit', not in its other meaning of stupid, a bit slow on the uptake.

Thieves notoriously conspire and plot together, and devise secret languages so that they can discuss their business in a code that will not be understood by others – a slang or jargon that used to be known as 'thieves' Latin'. Cockney rhyming slang itself was originally a closed language to the uninitiated and was created by crafty East Londoners to outwit authority and eavesdroppers.

'As thick as thieves' was already a common saying by the time it was first used in print in the 1800s, and we now use it primarily to describe people who are close friends.

TO THROW IN THE SPONGE

To throw in, or throw up, the sponge means to give up, to admit defeat. The metaphor is from prize-fighting, which predated modern boxing, and refers to a second from the boxer's corner tossing a sponge, used to refresh his contestant in between rounds, towards the centre of the ring, to signify that his man is beaten.

'To throw in the towel' also means to concede defeat in boxing, for a second might also literally throw a towel into the ring to show that the game is up.

TO THROW ONE'S HAT INTO THE RING

To enter a contest or to become a candidate for office. This expression relates to the early nineteenth-century custom of throwing one's hat into the boxing ring to indicate that you wanted to take on the pugilist.

By the early twentieth century, the term was regularly used in professional boxing and in 1912 it became firmly linked to political ambition when Theodore Roosevelt announced his intention to run for the presidency by telling a reporter: 'My hat's in the ring, the fight is on and I'm stripped to the buff.'

TOO MANY COOKS SPOIL
THE BROTH

A well-known proverb meaning that too many opinions on a matter become self-defeating. The adage has been in use since the sixteenth century, if not before.

For almost every proverb or nugget of wisdom, however, there is usually another that means precisely the opposite: the usual riposte for 'too many cooks spoil the broth' being 'many hands make light work'.

> *Groucho Marx (1895–1977) once commented: 'I'm going to stop asking my cooks to prepare broth for me. Over the years, I've found that too many broths spoil the cook.'*

TO TURN THE TABLES

To reverse a situation and put one's opponent in the predicament that one has been suffering. The saying was recorded in the early seventeenth century and was applied to the game of backgammon, the table or board on which it was played being known as 'the tables'.

The phrase may come from the old rumoured custom of reversing the table, or board, in games of chess or draughts, so that the opponents' relative positions are altogether changed – but even then it had a figurative meaning too.

In a sermon published in 1632, an English deacon called Robert Sanderson (1587–1663), who later became the Bishop of Lincoln, said:

Whosover thou art that dost another wrong, do but turn the tables: imagine thy neighbor were now playing thy game, and thou his.

A TURN-UP FOR THE BOOKS

A piece of luck or unexpected good fortune, or a surprising turn of events. This phrase comes from the world of betting on the horses.

The 'book' is the record of bets laid on a race and is naturally kept by a 'book'maker, commonly known as a bookie. When the horses do not run to form and the favourite does not win, it's a good day for the bookie and he can line his pockets; for him it's 'a turn-up[wards] for the books'.

UNDER THE COUNTER

This phrase originated during the Second World War, and describes a – then very common – practice among tradesmen with an eye to the main chance.

From the outbreak of the war, many items, ranging from the basics like eggs, butter, meat and jam to 'luxuries' such as petrol, silk stockings and chocolate, were rationed. Dishonest tradesmen would keep articles and foodstuffs that were in short supply out of sight or 'under the counter', for sale to favoured customers, usually at inflated prices.

This form of trading was part of the thriving wartime black market, and the term is still used today to describe any illicit trading.

TO WALK THE PLANK

To be put to the supreme test or, worse, to be about to die.

'Walking the plank' is a nautical term for a punishment involving being made to walk blindfold and with bound hands along a plank suspended over the ship's side – one eventually lands up in the drink as shark food, if not drowned first. It was a pirate custom of disposing of prisoners at sea in the seventeenth century.

The practice is probably more familiar in fiction than in fact, however, since pirates would have been unlikely to kill off captives, who could have been sold as slaves or ransomed.

In R. L. Stevenson's (1850–94) novel The Master of Ballantrae *(1889), James Durie and Colonel Francis Burke enlist with the pirates who capture their ship, but the brigands make their other prisoners walk the plank.*

The infamous Captain Hook, in J. M. Barrie's (1860–1937) Peter Pan and Wendy *(1912), meanwhile, threatened to flog Wendy and the Lost Boys with a cat-o'-nine-tails … and then make them walk the plank.*

THE WALLS HAVE EARS

This is a warning to watch what you say, or what secrets you divulge, wherever you are, because someone might be listening.

In the time of Catherine de'Medici (1519–89), wife of Henry II of France, certain rooms in the Louvre Palace, Paris, were said to be constructed to conceal a network of listening tubes called *auriculaires*, so that what was said in one room could be clearly heard in another. This was how the suspicious queen discovered state secrets and plots.

The legend of Dionysus's ear may also have been the inspiration for the phrase. Dionysus was a tyrant of Syracuse (see **the sword of Damocles**, page 171) in 431–367 BC, and his so-called 'ear' was a large ear-shaped underground cave cut into rock. It was connected to another chamber in such a way that he could overhear the conversations of his prisoners.

TO WASH ONE'S HANDS OF SOMETHING

To abandon something, to have nothing to do with some matter or person, or to refuse to take responsibility.

The allusion is to Pontius Pilate's washing of his hands after the trial of Jesus. Pilate was the Roman Governor of Judaea (AD 26–36) who tried Jesus. Although he found Christ not guilty, he washed his hands of the matter by bowing to the pressure of Jewish religious leaders and letting them decide Christ's fate:

> When Pilate saw that he could prevail nothing, but that rather a tumult was made, he took water, and washed his hands before the multitude, saying, I am innocent of the blood of this just person: see ye to it.
>
> Matthew 27:24

WHAM, BAM, THANK YOU, MA'AM

This rather vulgar euphemism for quick, meaningless sex was originally used by American forces during the Second World War.

The phrase was later employed – mostly by women – to describe short and unfulfilling sexual intercourse, or perhaps a one-night stand which had left them feeling used.

It is now used contemptuously for any selfish act of male gratification at women's expense.

WHAT A CARVE UP

This is an English slang phrase meaning to spoil someone's chances, or to have all prospects ruined.

In criminal circles, a 'carve up' means to share out illicit booty, while in New Zealand, it means to have bested everyone else, as in, 'He carved up in the snooker contest.'

The phrase is taken from the title of a 1961 spoof horror film starring Sid James (1913–76) and Shirley Eaton (1937–), in which family members gather at a haunted house to hear the reading of a will. The title made use of the double meaning of 'carve up' to refer both to the dividing of the inheritance and to a more literal 'carving up' of the victims, as members of the party are methodically picked off and gruesomely murdered.

Jonathan Coe (1961–) published a satirical novel of the same name in 1994: it concerns the greed prevalent in 1980s Britain, including the 'carving up' of state assets (see **to sell off the family silver**, page 149).

On the road, the phrase means to cut aggressively in front of another driver, one of the actions that has led to the phenomenon of 'road rage'.

There are now all sorts of 'rage' situations to describe the frustrations of modern life, such as 'trolley rage' in the supermarket, or 'air rage', as demonstrated by drunken passengers on aeroplanes.

WHAT IS SAUCE FOR THE GOOSE IS SAUCE FOR THE GANDER

This old phrase seems to promote sexual equality long before it was fashionable. It suggests that the same rules apply in both cases – what is fitting for the husband should also be fitting for the wife – though it is more likely that the phrase was used more generally to mean what is good enough for one person is good enough for another.

Originally, 'sauce', from the Latin *salsus*, meant salted food used as a relish with meat, such as pickled roots and herbs. 'Sauce' these days also means 'cheek' or 'impertinence', perhaps in relation to the piquancy of such relishes.

WHAT THE DICKENS?

An exclamation of surprise or disbelief, akin to 'What the devil?' The phrase is often shortened to 'What the . . .?' and in these modern times, 'f**k' is sometimes substituted as the last word.

'Dickens' here is probably a euphemism – one possibly in use since the sixteenth century – for the Devil, otherwise known as Satan or the Prince of Evil, and has nothing to do with the novelist Charles Dickens (1812–70).

In Low German, its equivalent is 'De duks!', which may have become altered in English to 'dickens'.

The phrase was already in use by the time Shakespeare was writing:

I cannot tell what the dickens his name is.

The Merry Wives of Windsor (1600; 3:2)

'To play the dickens' is an old-fashioned expression meaning to be naughty, or act like a devil.

WHERE THERE'S MUCK, THERE'S BRASS

An encouraging phrase to make one roll up one's sleeves and get to work, otherwise a statement that where there is dirt, there is money. Feeding the soil, harvesting the crops, mining the coal may make your hands dirty, but they can produce untold riches.

The saying has come to be associated with the grimy mining and manufacturing industries of the north of England, many of which brought their owners substantial wealth following the Industrial Revolution of the nineteenth century.

'Brass' is in fact a Yorkshire term for 'money', and this version of the phrase originated there – but the proverb *had* existed with a different wording since at least 1670, when John Ray (1627–1705) recorded 'Muck and money go together' in his collection of English proverbs.

WHERE'S THE BEEF?

Advertising slogan meets political catchphrase. The American Wendy hamburger chain's 1984 television commercial showed a group of elderly women looking at the small hamburger of a competitor on a huge bun – they all admired the bun, but the unimpressed third woman asked, 'Where's the beef?'

Later in 1984, when Walter Mondale (1928–) was seeking the Democratic presidential nomination, he famously quoted the slogan to describe what he thought was a lack of substance in the policies of his rival, Gary Hart (1936–).

In America, the phrase is also used to mean 'where's the problem?'

A WOLF IN SHEEP'S CLOTHING

Used to describe a malicious or dangerous person who uses a facade of innocence to fool others as to his or her true character.

The idea of such dissemblance has long been in circulation. One of the earliest phrases linking wolves and sheep comes from the Bible:

Beware of false prophets, which come to you in sheep's clothing, but inwardly they are ravening wolves.

Matthew 7:15

The original source of the phrase, however, is thought to be Aesop's fables, written in the sixth century BC. In the story, a wolf who is hunting sheep realizes that he can get close to the flock by disguising himself with a sheep's skin. But once he is among them, the shepherd – looking for a sheep to kill for his supper – mistakes the wolf for a suitable sheep and cuts its throat.

The moral of the story is that the wrongdoer will be punished by his own deceit.

TO BE WORTH ONE'S SALT

'Salt' is a significant euphemism, from the early nineteenth century onwards, for one's financial worth, as a play on the word 'salary', or the amount one earned.

In Roman times, a soldier received part of his pay in the form of a *salarium*, or salary, which was actually an allowance for the purchase of salt (the Latin for 'salt' is *sal*). Salt was not easily obtainable then, and a soldier was not 'worth his salt' if he did not **come up to scratch** (see page 53) – that is, did not deserve his *salarium*.

Consequently, to be 'true to one's salt' is to be loyal to your employers, those who pay your salary, or to maintain or stand by one's personal honour.

THE WRITING ON THE WALL

This is not graffiti, but a bad sign, a portent, often foreshadowing trouble or disaster.

The metaphor is biblical in origin and comes from Daniel 5:5–31, where King Belshazzar, while he was feasting, found out about the forthcoming destruction of the Babylonian Empire through the mysterious appearance of handwriting on a wall.

The words read in Aramaic, *mene, mene, tekel, upharsin*: literally, 'counted, weighed, divided'. Daniel interpreted these words as, 'You have been weighed in the balance and found wanting,' thereby predicting the King's downfall and that of his empire.

Indeed, Belshazzar was killed that night, and his kingdom was conquered.

YOU ARE WHAT YOU EAT

An informal slogan with 'alternative-lifestyle' overtones that dates back to the 1960s. Today, the phrase is associated with nutrition adviser Gillian McKeith (1959–), whose former popular TV show of the same name gained notoriety for McKeith's cheery analysis of her clients' bowel movements.

The idea behind the phrase, however, is far from new. In *Psychologie du Goût* (1825), the great philosopher of French cooking Anthelme Brillat-Savarin (1755–1826) wrote, 'Tell me what you eat and I will tell you what you are,' while in 1945, the diarist Sir Henry 'Chips' Channon (1897–1958) fondly commented on the death of Sir Harcourt Johnstone (1895–1945), Liberal MP, bon vivant and Minister for Overseas Trade:

He dug his grave with his teeth.

YOU CAN'T MAKE A SILK PURSE OUT OF A SOW'S EAR

Don't attempt to make something good or of great value from what is naturally bad or inferior in quality. A similar old proverb is 'you cannot make a horn out of a pig's ear'.

To make a pig's ear of something is to bodge it; the ear of a slaughtered pig being its most worthless part, no good for anything.

This ancient phrase was already a proverb by the mid 1500s and over time has inspired similar slang expressions, thought to have been instigated in the 1920s, such as 'to make a dog's breakfast' or 'dog's dinner' out of something.